D1238701

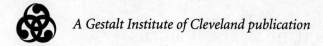 *A Gestalt Institute of Cleveland publication*

Getting Beyond Sobriety

Michael Craig Clemmens

Getting Beyond Sobriety

Clinical Approaches to Long-Term Recovery

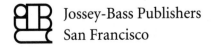
Jossey-Bass Publishers
San Francisco

A Gestalt Institute of Cleveland publication

Substantial discounts on bulk quantities of Jossey-Bass books are available to corporations, professional associations, and other organizations. For details and discount information, contact the special sales department at Jossey-Bass Inc., Publishers (415) 433–1740; Fax (800) 605–2665.

For sales outside the United States, please contact your local Simon & Schuster International office.

Jossey-Bass Web address: http://www.josseybass.com

 Manufactured in the United States of America on Lyons Falls Turin Book. This paper is acid-free and 100 percent totally chlorine-free.

Library of Congress Cataloging-in-Publication Data

Clemmens, Michael Craig
   Getting beyond sobriety: clinical approaches to long-term recovery/Michael Craig Clemmens.—1st ed.
     p. cm.—(The Jossey-Bass psychology series)
   Includes bibliographical references and index.
   ISBN 0–7879–0840–1
   1. Substance abuse—Treatment. 2. Gestalt therapy. I. Title. II. Series.
   [DNLM: 1. Alcoholism—psychology. 2. Alcoholism—rehabilitation.
   3. Temperance. WM 274 C626g 1997]
   RC564.C54 1997
   616.86'106—dc21
                                                    96–47105

FIRST EDITION
HB Printing 10 9 8 7 6 5 4 3 2 1

⟶ Contents

92786

For Ellen O'Brien Gaiser

May you Dance the happy road to destiny

—∿— **Preface**

As I sit with David in my office on a cold winter day, snow is falling outside. He's talking about how different his relationships have become in this, his tenth year of sobriety, and in particular about his feeling of being different at AA meetings. "I don't know what to talk about with some people anymore. When I first got sober I was always able to connect with other recovering addicts around how I drank and got high . . . what a junkie I was."

I ask David to stay with the difference in his experience now: Can he picture himself at the AA meeting talking to these people? He continues to speak, while beginning to rub his forehead as if to revive himself.

"There are so many other things I want to talk about at the meeting . . . the election, my difficulty being a father, the images I see when I meditate; but I feel I have to remain in that room and talk about the assigned topic . . . it makes me feel trapped." His eyes begin to tear up and he slowly shakes his head. "Things are different . . . I'm different."

I am listening to David and I feel touched by his struggle to make meaning of his changing experience. It's clear to me that he's in a different place than he was ten years ago. He's developed from a man whose main concern was to keep alcohol and drugs out of his body to a man who is looking at larger systems in life than his own skin boundary. How can I attend to this difference, yet honor the ground that he has walked over to get here?

This is the challenge of therapy with long-term recovering addicts: to attend to the changing contours of identity and relationships that evolve over time, while still valuing the foundation of what they've already accomplished. I have an image of an expanding membrane that encompasses more and more of life, and of David sitting inside it, gazing out and around. As I look again at the snow falling, I realize that I need to be inside this membrane with him. I sit cross-legged on the floor with David. I am appreciating again that recovery from addiction is more than a movement away from the drug. David's stage of recovery is an expansion, a development out into the world.

As I describe David, I'm reminded of all the other addicts I have known: sober and using, free and incarcerated, some still alive today and some long dead. For over twenty years, I've worked in some context with addicts—in detoxification and rehabilitation centers, in halfway houses, and in private practice. At times, I've worked with undiagnosed addicts in psychiatric settings. Through this time I have known hundreds of addicts, most of whom have returned to using drugs. Many of these people have been jailed or hospitalized, or have died from their addiction. Most of the addicts I have known do not recover; most either continue to use drugs or relapse after some period of abstinence.

This book is the product of my two decades of involvement in addiction and recovery treatment. My own personal experience is that I've been in recovery from alcohol and drug addiction for more than twenty years. One of the questions that I've asked myself during these years is, What is recovery? Initially, in my own recovery and in my work with others, I thought of recovery as sobriety or abstinence, a kind of repression, a *not-doing*. As I stayed in recovery, however, I experienced my own growth in recovery and saw others focused on themes beyond sobriety. My clinical experience is that recovering addicts who come to therapy face numerous other issues and impasses *in addition* to abstinence. These life issues or impasses are similar and include those that all people experience.

The differences with recovering addicts are twofold. First, issues and impasses occur in the addict's life within the context of a pattern of self-modulation. *Self-modulation* is an individual's pattern of influencing the amount and degree of contact that he or she has at any given moment. The addict's pattern of self-modulation is one of avoidance and desensitization based on moving away from sensation to action. This movement is accomplished by using alcohol or drugs, thus decreasing or modulating the sensations felt. This pattern often continues long into recovery. It is accomplished by using means other than drugs to shift from sensation to action without much awareness. The pattern remains the dominant option for the addict in interaction with others and the world at large until new patterns are developed. Second, the long-term effects of using drugs change awareness and create gaps in the addict's psychosocial development. These two impacts of addiction result in addicts entering recovery with a limited range of contact skills and internal capacities. In this book, I address how these differences affect an addict's recovery as well as how they affect my own theory and practice of clinical work.

The small minority of addicts I have known who remain in recovery appear to have developed new capacities for living with themselves and with others. The development of these capacities tends to evolve in stages, with individual differences. These stages begin with the task of maintaining abstinence and evolve through various levels of interpersonal and personal development with the potential of transcendence as the ultimate development. This development can be supported and enhanced in therapy. The particular challenges of each stage of recovery become the basis for continuing in recovery. My intention in this book is to describe these developing capacities in recovering addicts and offer a Gestalt therapy approach to identifying the client's particular struggle in recovery.

When I first began to work in addiction treatment, the approved models or approaches were dominated by the influence of Alcoholics Anonymous and by the encounter techniques used in facilities such as Synanon, Daytop, and the facility where I worked, White Deer Run in Allenwood, Pennsylvania. In that setting, I experienced both the power of the therapeutic milieu and the unattended range and diversity of the individuals in treatment. Much of the treatment was highly experiential, employing enactment of individuals' defensive behaviors in an effort to get them to stop playing games and admit to their addiction. We also did some substantive work helping addicts to work through painful experiences and to adopt socially responsible behaviors.

What amazed me about this experience was how few patients remained abstinent even six months later. One thing we must always deal with in working with recovering addicts is relapse. Terence Gorski and Merlene Miller have drawn attention to this constant reality and described treatment approaches for dealing with relapsing or relapsed clients. My experience is that relapse is often a gradual process that only culminates with the use of the drug. The progressive reversion to the addiction style of contact and self-modulation begins a long time before the addict actually uses that first drug. In Chapter Seven, I will address this process with case examples.

Over time, the *disease model* has become the primary model in working with addiction. This theory originated with Alcoholics

Anonymous, was later approved by the American Medical Association, and was furthered by the typological research of E. M. Jellinek. The American Psychiatric Association's *Diagnostic and Statistical Manual* (fourth edition) presents the most current version of the disease model, describing addiction as substance "dependence" and as a list of observable behaviors, including indications of physiological tolerance and decrease in social functioning. It is a perspective that conceives of the addict as suffering from a disease in the manner that one can suffer from a physical illness such as diabetes.

I have found this model inadequate in working with addicts for two reasons. First, the disease conception of addiction often supports clients in avoiding responsibility for their behavior. By placing the focus on some external process, an "it," addicts may refuse to own either their behavior when intoxicated or the benefits they derive from that behavior. Sometimes, even when sober, addicts explain their actions as "My disease is acting up." This kind of projection away from the self, coupled with the belief that "I can't help it," also decreases the addict's exploration of new behavioral options in recovery.

The second reason I have found this approach to be inadequate is its exclusive emphasis on abstinence. The oppositional focus on drinking versus abstinence supports the addict in living a binary life, and thus impedes the essential recognition that there is much more to life and recovery from addiction than abstinence. Yet I believe that the development of a greater, more expanded life is *based on the foundation of abstinence,* and that aspects of each addict's individual growth and restoration extend from this fundamental ground of sobriety. It is my further intention in this book to describe these processes of growth as recovery beyond sobriety.

Different life themes or issues seem to become salient for the addict at different times during recovery, and the sequence of these themes suggests a development of stages in the recovery process. What then is the need for another theory or approach to this extensive social problem and phenomenon? I believe there exists a need to bring our clinical understanding of *addicts in relation with their world* through the stages of recovery, particularly long-term recovery. As yet, there has been little writing or research on the experience of addicts in longer-term recovery. Even the main text of Alcoholics Anonymous was produced when the authors had been sober no more than five years. The literature of Narcotics Anonymous clearly defines addiction and the differences between addiction and recovery but does not elaborate the processes of accomplishing this change. These texts are self-help books and thus do not offer clinical approaches, only guidelines. As helpful as these programs are for their participants, they don't tend to be explicit about the development of capacities in recovery. This is a common aspect of both programs—much of what addicts do to change is not written; it is part of an oral and implicit tradition.

In an earlier article, I began to outline stages of addiction and recovery. That focus, which I will continue here, describes the addict's use of drugs as a coping strategy—what early Gestalt theorists Frederick Perls, Ralph Hefferline, and Paul Goodman called "creative adjustment." Each person has a style of interacting with others and attending to self, a pattern of modulating contact. This pattern or contact style becomes an habituated style of interacting in the world. It is a way of desensitizing the self, which leaves the addict with an inadequate repertoire of behaviors. I propose that for the addict, alcohol and drug use is a form of modulation of sensation that has interpersonal and intrapersonal advantages. The discomfort that intoxication temporarily obscures may precede the addict's period of drug use, and most certainly continues after abstinence. This model of addictive behavior is a combination of withdrawal-avoidance and social theories of addiction.

The overview or model of addiction recovery that I am presenting takes into consideration a second phenomenon: the individual differences that each addict as a human being brings to his or her life. This is consistent with the recent research according to Elizabeth Epstein and Barbara McGrady: "It can no longer be assumed that substance abuse is of a unitary nature and that substance abusers are a homogeneous lot." What is apparent to clinicians is how individual differences in levels of psychological development and personality organization, as well as racial, social, and ethnic differences, shape the issues and forms of each addict's recovery. With regard to development, we can see in our recovering clients two processes—one involving the more uniformly recognizable stages of recovery from addiction, and the other, the unique psychological development of each individual. Together, these processes are like prisms that reflect and offer different refractions of each other. Recovery is often the continuation of an interrupted developmental pattern.

In the addict's field of awareness, the idea or feeling of the drug and its resulting desensitization remain fixed as an option long after abstinence begins. Because of the long-term impact of drug use on emotions and identity, the addict's relationship with others and with self can remain intertwined with drug or alcohol use long into recovery.

Gestalt therapy offers a perspective that attends to ongoing individual and interpersonal dynamics. This Gestalt approach emphasizes contact at the multiple boundaries of the client's life, employing techniques for clarifying that boundary (techniques often misapplied by some addiction therapists), and creating a lens for viewing the experience of addicts both individually and within interpersonal systems. Examples of these multiple boundaries are the boundary that defines the relationship between self and a significant other, the boundary of a family the client is a part of and identifies with, and the boundary of the client's relationships with various social, cultural, and ethnic groups. This approach is intended to support clients like David who are developing and in transition—recovering addicts who come to therapy needing to develop skills for moving beyond sobriety and into a fuller life.

My intention here is to offer another approach to working with recovering addicts. I will provide case examples based on my own practice, including work in various treatment facilities and interviews with recovering addicts, and I will outline the salient principles of Gestalt therapy and how they relate to recovery.

ACKNOWLEDGMENTS

I want to acknowledge a number of people who supported me in the development of this book. The ideas and experiences described here are the result of my own recovery and my work with addicts in various settings. I want to thank the staff of White Deer Run Treatment Center from 1975 through 1978, most particularly Dick and Donna Flanagan, Judy Pollard (who gave me Joseph Zinker's book), Casey Nepa, Dennis Pratz, Jeff Cousins, Don Langraff, and Brett Hamilton. At the Butler "A" Center, I want to thank Ellen O'Brien Gaiser and Ben Krumpe, who helped me put the Gestalt approach to addiction into practice. My own recovery and belief in this work have been supported by Learita Garfield Scott and Coleman McG. I also want to thank Joseph Zinker for helping me get grounded and focused so I could begin this work.

I particularly want to acknowledge the support and direction I received from two mentors, Marjorie Creelman and Tom Cutolo, both deceased, whose sharp ideas and belief in me provided a strong path to follow and push against. I also want to thank all the addicts who as clients have taught me about recovery and reminded me of myself.

In the actual development of this book, I especially want to thank my editors from the Gestalt Institute of Cleveland Press, Gordon Wheeler and Jim Kepner, as well as Alan Rinzler from Jossey-Bass. Gordon, as always, provided enthusiastic support for my vision. Jim provided both critical editing and years of collaboration in teaching body-oriented therapy, which helped develop the sections of that approach in this book. Alan pushed me to make my ideas readable to the general reader, not an easy task. I also want to acknowledge Erin Simon for her early editing of this work and Barbara Edelman for her excellent editorial work on the final draft.

I want to acknowledge two of my colleagues at the Gestalt Institute of Cleveland, who supported the genesis of this book. I especially want to thank Edwin Nevis for his idea of staff development at GIC; this book is a product of that idea. And I also thank Mark McConville, who edited and nurtured my early article that is the basis for this book.

Finally, I want to thank my wife, Denise, and my children, Lindsey and Brenden, for their tolerance, love, and support during this project. This is clearly *our* book.

January 1997   Michael Craig Clemmens
                                                  Pittsburgh, Pennsylvania

Recommended Reading

Clemmens, M. (1993). Chemical dependency as a developed contact style. *Gestalt Review, 4* (1), 1–6.

Epstein, E., & McGrady, B. (1994). Research on the nature and treatment of alcoholism: Does one inform the other? *Journal of Consulting and Clinical Psychology, 62* (6), 1091–1095.

Jellinek, E. M. (1960). *The disease concept of alcoholism.* New Haven, CT: College and Universities Press.

Perls, F., Hefferline, R., & Goodman, P. (1951). *Gestalt therapy: Excitement and growth in the human personality.* New York: Julian Press.

CHAPTER ONE

Addiction and Gestalt Therapy

T his chapter presents a new model of addiction and recovery, the self-modulation model, contrasting this approach with the disease model, which is currently the most commonly used model in the treatment of addiction. It also presents the Gestalt approach to addiction and recovery employed throughout this book, which emphasizes the process of self-modulation from addiction through recovery. The patterns an individual develops before and during addiction change in recovery, being replaced by new patterns of behavior, new means of self-modulation. If we are to fully appreciate an addict's struggles during recovery, it is essential to frame the addict's changes in the context of previously developed patterns.

THE DISEASE MODEL

As described by Stanton Peele, the dominant model in the treatment of addiction is the disease model. It is rooted in the literature of Alcoholics Anonymous and described in the *Diagnostic and Statistical Manual* of the American Psychiatric Association as a progressive series of identifiable behaviors, including both alcohol or drug use and decreasing social functioning. One particular advantage of this model is that to describe addiction as an "it" lessens the addict's sense of shame. The addict is not described as *bad* but rather as suffering from a disease. Current research supports genetic correlates for addiction.

My intention here is not to dispute genetic predisposition but to help avoid the blurring of personal responsibility. If we understand addiction only as a genetic disease, we may fail to examine the possible limitations of the current style of treatment. Moreover, as therapists, we perhaps *interfere* with the important step in recovery of the addict's assuming responsibility for his or her own behavior.

There is a still larger problem with the disease model, or with any model of human development not based on the lived experience of subjects. The disease model is a *categorical construct,* an interpretation of behavior in terms of the previously existing framework of physical illnesses. This approach to addicts' behavior helps create an entity that is separate from the addict, a kind of lurking germ that may emerge at any moment to make the addict use drugs or alcohol. Such a projection can lead clinicians and recovering addicts away from a focus on behavior, meaning-making, and choices, and instead toward a focus on determining who has the disease.

THE SELF-MODULATION MODEL

Despite hunger, poverty, the threatened loss of family, job, or even life, addicts organize their experience around drug use to the virtual exclusion of all other interests and responsibilities. From a Gestalt perspective, the drug or drink remains dominant in the addict's awareness and is never finished or closed. Even when an addict is abstinent, the drug or other forms of desensitization continue to dominate. It is as if drinking or getting high is the only thing that matters to the addict; this exclusive relationship with the drug is the definition of addiction. While some addicts may not outwardly appear to be so focused on their drug, it is in fact the priority in their lives, after which they attend to other life issues.

This model is my attempt to provide what Elaine Kepner and Lois Brien call a "behavioristic phenomenology," a description of an addict's behavior as well as the meaning of that behavior. This model can thus provide both the "what" and the "what for" of addiction and recovery. It is a description of the progression of addiction as a process of self-modulation: how the addict modulates his or her own behavior. Through this regulation of behavior, addicts influence both their own experience and that of others. To view addiction as a self-modulation is to understand that it serves the addict in some ways, one of which is that individuals can influence and alter the sensations they experience, thus avoiding certain experiences that they find undesirable. Other ways that the addict's process serves him or her include ease in accomplishing tasks that might otherwise be difficult, a sustained sense of confluence or connection with others, and a sustained sense of self that feels coherent and integrated. These advantages can be perceived in the actual descriptions of active and recovering addicts.

The second aspect of the self-modulation model is my attempt to describe the addict's continuation of behaviors that appear to have diminishing returns. Addicts' persistence in using the same process (intoxication) results in a narrowing of their experienced world, a movement that has enormous negative impact on their interpersonal lives. This downside of chronic intoxication is what we usually define as addiction.

What then is the upside or advantage of the addict's persisting in a pattern of intoxication despite the subsequent narrowing of life experience? Often the ongoing preferred result for the addict is maintenance of the state of intoxication. Another way to put it is that addicts have a relationship with the drug that they know, value, and identify with, as with an interpersonal relationship. As one of my clients said of his choice of narcotics, "It's my wife and my life." The nature of this relationship is crucial in understanding and working with addicts in therapy. Without the perspective of self-modulation, any addict's behavior seems either to be a meaningless dysfunction or the symptom of some disease; the tasks of recovery, therefore, seem only remedial steps in changing the problem, rather than steps toward the development of contact skills and expanding levels of interpersonal relationship.

Being based on field theory, this model addresses differences among addicts as well as differences in field conditions not usually attended to in the disease model. According to Gordon Wheeler, *field theory* is a concept of Gestalt psychology that maintains that we experience our awareness within the larger field or environment that is already moving and changing. This larger environment includes other people, our present social, familial, or political situation, and other environmental conditions. But the individual organizes this field based on his or her need. This organization of the field is also based on the individual's development, personality, and individual factors. A ten-year-old boy and a thirty-year-old alcoholic organize the field of a bar in different ways. The boy focuses on and sees the bag of pretzels and the bright colors of the jukebox; the alcoholic focuses on and sees the bottles behind the bar, feels his thirst, and moves directly to the bar to order a drink. Because addicts vary in personality, developmental growth, age, gender, and other individual factors, the self-modulation model can help clarify how these differences organize the fields of both addiction and recovery. It will allow us to work with each addict individually, appreciating the unique intrapersonal and interpersonal struggles of each. These individual differences provide a context that can enlighten our understanding of the addict as a unique person, embedded in a life history and a relational world.

Finally, the self-modulation model describes the progression of addiction as a powerful influence on the addict. This allows us to consider how the addict's use of drugs may influence that person's level of functioning in recovery. What this adds to our understanding as therapists is that we recognize stages of recovery as an incremental restoration and development of the addict's social and psychological integration.

OVERVIEW OF GESTALT THERAPY

While there have recently been some efforts to describe a Gestalt perspective in working with addiction, the literature of Gestalt therapy overall has devoted minimal attention to addiction treatment. Frederick Perls, Ralph Hefferline, and Paul Goodman saw alcoholism as muscularly anchored in oral development. They describe the drinker as wanting to drink his or her environment in, to "get easy and total confluence without the excitement (which to them is a painful effort) of contacting, destroying and assimilating." What does this intense and mechanical description mean? Perls and his colleagues were describing how addicts try to experience familiarity and comfort (confluence) without getting to know other people. This process of entering into novel situations, of meeting new people and thereby taking risks, is one that is by nature stimulating—emotionally, cognitively, and physically. Making contact involves listening, agreeing or disagreeing, noticing differences, and coming to experience both ourselves and others. Addicts, when using and in recovery, often try to avoid the experience of stimulation, sensing it as discomfort. Part of this pattern can result in a rush to reach familiarity.

The theory and practice of Gestalt therapy offer two options to addiction treatment that can be most useful. First, Gestalt therapy is a therapy of boundaries, one that focuses on the self-environment boundary as well as on boundaries within the self (split-off parts or polarities). This emphasis supports our observing the individual addict through different developmental stages of recovery and normal maturation. Psychological and emotional development is seen as a sequence or evolution of differing boundary relationships such as self–physical environment, self-parent, self-peers.

Second, Gestalt therapy views behavior as self-modulation, a view that allows us to understand the addict's behavior as *useful in some manner*; it is not only a potentially self-destructive habituation, it is also a coping style, a creative adjustment that enables addicts to tolerate stressful experiences. These experiences may be interpersonal or interactive, such as job interviews, first meetings in a social context, or conflicts with family members. They may also be intrapersonal, primarily within the self, such as facing painful memories or experiencing sadness or frustration. In addiction, this process, which starts as a useful modulation, develops into a pattern of behavior for its own sake. That is, the addict develops the pattern of using drugs so that the reasons for the drug's usefulness cease to be part of the user's awareness, until eventually his or her awareness is only of the drug itself. It is only when the addict stops using that the previously avoided feelings and situations are again experienced.

Organismic Self-Regulation

In Gestalt therapy, the term *organismic self-regulation* denotes the process of our recognizing what is most useful to us in any given situation and of choosing to act or not act on that recognition. We organize our perceptual, cognitive, and kinesthetic experience into meaningful and needful wholes or figures. In normal functioning, this organizing process leads us to the figures that are most useful to us. For example, when hungry we may think of restaurants that serve the type of food we crave, and we crave the food that satisfies whatever nutrients we need. Thus, what is *figural*—what stands out for us more sharply than all other possible figures—is ideally what we require in the moment.

In addiction, the organic process of feeling or seeing what is most necessary becomes skewed. Instead, the alcohol or drug becomes fixed as the uppermost figure in the addict's experience, to the exclusion of other relevant needs, impeding and possibly halting social and emotional development. In fact, other figures are not salient; the addict does not see them. The addict craves drugs when hungry, alcohol when desiring companionship, and cocaine when needing to pay the bills. This is the nature of addiction, to eventually blot out the rest of life. But the addict's focus on the drug is also based on a need: the need to maintain self and a particular frame of meaning. As J. Richard White describes, addiction is both "an attempt at survival, specifically spiritual survival" and "a desire for a meaningful life." My experience of working with addicts is that people who become addicted are seeking something more than daily existence, but they end up lost and unable to achieve that which they pursue. By their choice of a drug solution, addicts limit their own horizons and possibilities. I believe it is our task, as therapists working with addicts, to appreciate not only the limiting aspects of the addict's relationship with drugs, but also the meaningful survival functions such a relationship creates. This perspective will allow us greater vision in working with contact issues in recovery.

The Gestalt approach to addiction is based on three observations: First, addiction is defined as the addict's exclusive relationship with the drug, making other relationships or contact secondary and peripheral. Second, this relationship that the addict has with the drug both serves as an avoidance of other sensations and constitutes an attempt at meaningful survival. And third, any approach to working with addicts needs to address both the meaning of the addict's survival behavior and the metapattern of avoiding fuller contact with the self and the environment.

I want to present several principles of Gestalt therapy as frameworks for illuminating the process of addiction and recovery. They are process and descriptive principles rather than content oriented. In addiction and recovery, the drug is the content, and patterns of behavior are the processes that need to be supported or altered. What I believe to be more important is what the addict does, what that action accomplishes and means for him or her. Attending to the addict's process provides us with access to these behaviors and meanings. In working with addicts in long-term recovery, we often see that the drug or drink may be absent but the individual's process may continue unchecked, leading almost inevitably to relapse into overt addictive behavior.

Cycle of Experience

In identifying this metapattern of drug use as the dominant interest (or figure) for addicts, I have found it useful to work with the process by which this constant desire or thought occurs. This fixed pattern is what differentiates the addict from the nonaddict—from someone who is hungry and eats rather than drinks, who opens a bill and pays it rather than using drugs. A useful model for illustrating this development of a rising need (figure) and its resulting behavioral action is the *cycle of experience* as developed by Joseph Zinker and others at the Gestalt Institute of Cleveland. We can see the cycle in its uninterrupted form as a continuous movement from ground to figure and back again to ground, from vague sensation to specific object of attention and from increasing to decreasing flow of energy. Two examples of this cycle will provide clarification:

A man is watching television and begins to feel a vague gnawing sensation in his stomach. He initially ignores the sensation, but soon feels it again and recognizes it as hunger. He thinks to himself, "I am hungry." He wonders what he might eat and begins to picture a piece of chicken in his refrigerator. He moves to the kitchen, opens the refrigerator, and takes out the chicken. As he eats the chicken, his stomach muscles relax and he eventually feels full. He sits back down in front of the television, his feeling of hunger having passed, and his attention returns to the movie.

A woman is going through a stack of photographs. She sifts through them casually until she comes across the photo of a friend who recently died of cancer. As she looks at the photo, her breathing deepens and she feels her throat tighten. She feels as if she can't put down the photo; it is the sole object of her attention. Beginning to cry, she stares at the photograph, and whispers under her breath, "Oh Mary, I miss you!" She weeps more fully, relaxing her throat. Feeling as if she needs to talk to someone, to not be alone with this sadness, she phones her sister and tells her what she misses about Mary. After a few minutes, her grief passes. She ends her conversation with her sister and returns to sorting her photographs, which she can now attend to.

This is the normal human process of experiencing ourselves and others. Our energy increases as our interest becomes a clear figure; we act upon what or who interests us (figure) and make contact with it or them. Having done this, we integrate these experiences as part of our ground. My intention in presenting this cycle is to describe the process as a unit of experience, an experiential snapshot of how we behave. But the context or ground out of which any feelings or needs become interesting is important to this process. The figure of our interest always stands in relation to the ground; nothing meaningful exists in and of itself.

During this cycle, energy rises in a kind of excitement. If for some reason (fear, shame, a belief that we won't get what we are interested in) we block or inhibit our energy or interest, then our excitement becomes anxiety. The diagram in Figure 1.1 identifies rising energy in the first half or left-hand side of the cycle. Telfair-Richards has identified this high energy in support of action as Yang, while Yin is the *falling energy* that supports assimilation and movement toward what Frederick Perls called "zero point." The ability to tolerate and stay with either of these types of energy can be thought of as a diagnostic or assessment of a person's contact functioning. We all have different preferences for these frequencies in relation to our own history (ground) and style.

Addicts tend to try to get to the middle of the cycle quickly, avoiding the slow rising of energy that exists in most everyday situations. Intoxication from drugs allows the addict to shorten this period by moving to action. Conversely, as addicts continue in their frequent usage, they have less tolerance for the second half of this cycle, less tolerance for the slower pace of making meaning or of integrating an experience. This is particularly true when the experience an addict has come through is an embarrassing or painful one.

Addiction as a Developed Contact Style

As the addict progresses through the stages of addiction, the flow of the cycle is consistently modified and parts of the cycle are skipped or barely experienced. Figure 1.2 illustrates how the addict's experience becomes modified. The narrower ellipse depicts the shorter amount

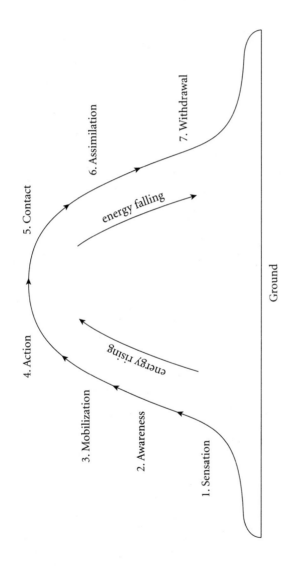

Figure 1.1. "Ideal" Cycle of Experience.

Source: Adapted from Kepner, J. I. *Body Process: Working with the Body in Psychotherapy.* San Francisco: Jossey-Bass, 1993, p. 91.

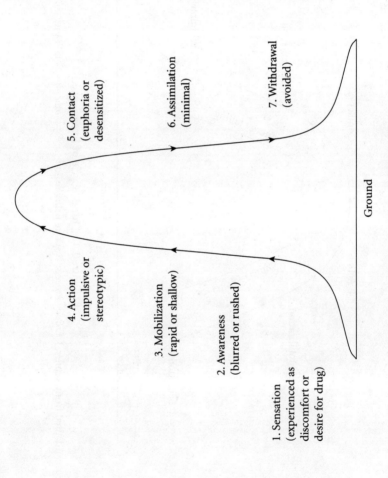

5. Contact
(euphoria or
desensitized)

6. Assimilation
(minimal)

7. Withdrawal
(avoided)

4. Action
(impulsive or
stereotypic)

3. Mobilization
(rapid or shallow)

2. Awareness
(blurred or rushed)

1. Sensation
(experienced as
discomfort or
desire for drug)

Ground

Figure 1.2. Addiction Cycle.

of time and attention given to accurately developing sensation, choosing an action, and to integrating and assimilating the experience.

The addict tends to move from sensation (1) to action (4) and back again repeatedly. It is a sensation-action loop. An example might be an addict who gets on an airplane without any thought of drinking. He begins to feel nervous, orders a drink, and downs it without thinking. Having felt little effect from the first drink, he quickly orders another and downs it in one gulp. The addict feels a sensation (nervousness), does not try to understand it, gives no thought to his pledge not to drink again, and acts almost instinctively *twice* before he realizes he is nearly intoxicated. This jumping into the cycle becomes like hot-wiring a car, bypassing the normal starting mechanism so that an action occurs abruptly without preliminary orientation.

The addict rushes through the orienting parts of experience—awareness (2) and mobilization (3)—creating a kind of immediate or impulsive pattern of action. Any contradictory information that might lead to a different action, such as memory of the last drinking episode, doesn't emerge into the addict's awareness. In the movement back to sensation, the contact functions of assimilation (6) and withdrawal (7) are shortened or avoided. This results in addicts' learning little from their experience. What supports this lack of withdrawal and assimilation is that the addict is intoxicated, cognitively dulled, and thus less aware of feelings other than drug effects. In the example of the man on the airplane, after realizing that he is drinking again, the addict says to himself, "What difference does it make? I'm already drunk."

The addiction cycle represents a contact style that eventually funnels all experiences though the same action, that is, drinking or using drugs. Addiction is a mobilization of energy through the wrong action. I am reminded of the stories told by addicts about how they needed to be high in order to sleep, eat, make love, drive a car, or get through any of the other essentials of life.

Each addict's progression can be understood by how the individual addict develops this kind of pattern of contact. They may experience themselves and others in this pattern from early in life, and in such cases, drug use becomes a continuation of the pattern of avoidance; the drug facilitates a pattern of rapid movement from sensation to action. This is especially true of addicts who begin their drug use in adolescence, a period of development during which the self is embedded in the family and environment, and particularly in the patterns of making contact. Use of drugs or alcohol, which may lessen the awkwardness and confusion so prevalent during adolescence, can strengthen or exaggerate the already existing sensation-action patterns characteristic of this turbulent period.

The addiction cycle illustrates not only the behavior of most addicts while using, but a potentially fixed pattern of behavior during recovery as well; that is, it can be a useful template for understanding the ways in which addicts organize their experience when not drinking or using. It offers a map of the moment-to-moment contact style of the abstinent yet not fully recovered addict. In recovery, this cycle can represent the addict's avoidance of new situations by quickly moving away from feelings to action. Common examples of this kind of reflexive action include labeling feelings or experience prematurely or substituting another substance (food) or behavior (sex, overwork) for the original feeling or need. This addiction pattern—the fundamental conflict of intolerance of sensation—continues into recovery unless addressed, resulting in an isolated self and a limited emotional life. In later recovery, addicts who maintain this pattern may remain self-preoccupied and glib about life. They may seem to have answers to everything, but to have limited interests; to know how to handle problems but not know how to connect with others.

Throughout this book, I refer to this addiction pattern of self-modulation. The restoration that occurs in recovery is the result of changing this pattern and moving it to a fuller cycle of contact (as in Figure1.1.

Restoring Capacities for Contact

What can be restored or developed in recovery are the capacities for contact—the varying experiences of interrelationship with others. But what of the addict's capacities for participation in these different relationships? Does abstinence alone support the addict to become a father, mother, team member, or even to see him or herself in any of these roles?

It is my contention that as addiction progresses, the addict moves to awareness of increasingly smaller levels of system, until eventually experiencing only him or herself. Conversely, we can think of recovery from addiction as the addict's growth in awareness of, and inclusion in, larger and larger levels of system. This is the essence of long-term recovery as relational growth: the addict's increasing capacity to identify and attend to ever larger levels of system beyond self.

As an example of both the narrowing of contact during addiction and the expansion of involvement with others during recovery, consider Diane. At the age of twenty-one, Diane was an honors student at college, involved in numerous activities, and busy socially both at school and with her family. Upon graduation, she began to drink regularly with fellow professionals at parties and after work. Her drinking, which started slowly, eventually consumed more and more of her time. She stopped associating with her college friends because they weren't cool (didn't drink often) and she socialized exclusively with those who did drink. Her work began to suffer and she rarely visited her family, saying, "I don't have any time." While such a separation might certainly be a normative stage for a young professional woman, the truth in this case was that Diane was busy drinking. Her other relationships took increasingly less focus, and she moved toward spending longer periods of time by herself. Her main interest and relationship had become maintaining a certain level of intoxication.

When Diane stopped drinking, her main focus continued to be on herself: how not to drink when she thought about alcohol all the time. To stay abstinent, she began to attend AA women's meetings. Initially, she could only tolerate a *dyadic* or one-to-one relationship, but eventually she started to see herself as a member of a group. Her withdrawal from other systems, which had progressed while she was drinking, gradually reversed. She saw herself more in relation to others; moreover, the quality of these relationships was different, a change that could only have been accomplished by her developing capacity to interact at deeper levels.

Diane is an example of the impact of an addict's drug use on her capacity for involvement in an expanding interpersonal field. When considering the behavior and potential treatment focus for addicts, it is helpful for us to consider *level of system,* by which I refer to the levels of complexity of relationships. Gestalt therapy offers a framework of multiple levels of system through which we can look at addiction, beginning with the level of self (intrapersonal), and extending to the transpersonal level. My experience and belief is that this movement outward from the self to include larger levels of system constitutes psychological development. To have a solid sense of self and to then expand one's field beyond the self requires the development of certain contact skills. The progression of addiction is the shrinking of one's field to self, and the impediment to movement beyond the level of self.

Levels of System

To delineate these concepts, I have expanded on the levels of system and development described by Mary Ann Huckabay and Ken Wilber. As health professionals, we can use levels of system to identify particular boundaries where the addict encounters dilemmas. This perspective can help us to diagnose the client's impasses, and can thus guide our therapeutic interventions.

INTRAPERSONAL. According to Huckabay, this level can be defined as "dynamics and properties that pertain within the boundaries of the self-system." The importance of looking at the addict at the intrapersonal level is that the boundary of the self (I–not I) can be described in terms of its qualities, such as porous and flexible or rigid and impenetrable.

When we attend to addicts on the intrapersonal level, the initial work is to help them define their boundary in relation to drugs and alcohol. As this boundary is defined, we can work with addicts to attend to definition or identity, to the qualities or parts within them, and to their own sensations. An example of this last task is to help addicts in recovery to identify and distinguish sensations as other than cues for using drugs and alcohol. An addict may experience irritation or nervousness as "wanting to get high." With support for staying with this sensation, the addict might recognize the experienced irritation as fear or anger about a recent event.

Another example of working with addicts at the intrapersonal boundary is to help them learn to slow down their pace. Many addicts react rather than act; their movement around the cycle is rapid even in recovery. By developing self-modulating skills such as breathing and grounding, addicts can influence their own level of anxiety and thus learn not to react habitually.

INTERPERSONAL. As the addict begins to move on in recovery, he or she moves from the exclusive preoccupation with self to interacting with others. The field created by this interaction establishes a boundary that can be described in terms of a process of give and take; differences, polarities, and collaborative roles support this process. For example, the relationship between an addict and his or her partner is an interpersonal system. The two people develop a pattern of interacting, and each person experiences the other person. Another important step at the interpersonal level is the point at which an addict reaches out to first seek help or treatment. The interpersonal relationship is the model of AA sponsorship. This is often difficult for the recovering addict whose sense of self with others is frequently shame based. The other characteristic of interpersonal relationships for addicts is a sense of mistrust.

In working with addiction, therapist and client become an interpersonal level of system. The therapist can help the client see their shared interaction as an example of how the client behaves or interacts with others. In later recovery, addicts have traditionally developed some skills at interacting with others, a development that involves working through the feelings of personal shame and mistrust of other people.

GROUP OR FAMILY LEVEL. Through intention and interaction, multiple selves form a larger whole or system. The qualities of the system can vary according to boundary, communication patterns, and norms. From this perspective, the group, family, or system is the organizing lens, and for the therapist, the group or family is the client. For individuals who experience themselves as part of this system, relatedness and common goals are more salient than for those who do not.

The group level denotes the interaction and relationships between all members of the group or family. It is larger than the sum of its parts. The group creates its own boundary, its own definition of who is a member. For addicts in recovery, being part of a group can constitute an important element in the healing process. Working at the group level allows the client to explore the meaning and experiences of being "part of." Frequently, addicts view groups as wanting to control them, and therefore resist involvement. This is the struggle some addicts have with AA or NA; they see joining such a group as a threat of being swallowed up or of losing their individual identity.

Because of shared history, families constitute a unique group, a unique type of larger system. I include family as part of group level because the challenge for addicts to integrate and identify with a group is often based on their earliest experience of a larger system, that is, their family. Many of us working with addicts in recovery see the addict's family of origin as an important template of his or her behavior throughout recovery. The addict's family is often the model for how he or she perceives the self in groups.

COMMUNITY LEVEL. As addicts continue to expand their field beyond the self, they become part of a community of others, such as a town, ethnic group, race, or nation. This level is analogous to Mark

McConville's "tribe" level of relationship in development. Individuals may be aware of or feel connected to any of these groups, which are interrelated and are an extension of the self into the world.

An example of this level of system for addicts is involvement in the local community, through service work or social action. Another significant level to attend to, in working with addicts, involves their identification with an ethnic and racial group. This issue is often neglected by counselors, or considered to be out of the province of psychotherapy, but as addicts continue to grow in recovery, they may need to work in therapy to define this experience.

TRANSPERSONAL AND SPIRITUAL. I think of this level of interaction as both beyond and inclusive of the body, individual identity, and group. The transpersonal is the process of holding all systems in awareness at the same time: perceiving the connection of different groups, and reaching beyond the self while still maintaining a self. A person's ability to perceive all these levels as interrelated is highly field independent and transcendent. For the recovering addict, this is the level of awareness described in the eleventh and twelfth steps of Alcoholics Anonymous and Narcotics Anonymous. In my experience, it is rarely reached by addicts—or others, for that matter. While some form of spiritual belief exists in early recovery, the capacity to transcend self, groups, families, and ethnicity is the outcome of growth, and is thus more common in later recovery, after the addict has developed through the levels of system.

These levels of system are fields of relatedness in human experience. For addicts, they can range from fully developed to flat. By attending to these levels of system, therapists and consultants can locate sites for intervention, frames of reference for understanding addicts' behaviors, and the systems in which those behaviors are embedded. I believe we can see these levels as developmental stages for any individual. The movement from self to self-others is clearly a growth step, dependent on increasing toleration of contact with others. Each of these stages then continues, with each preceding step becoming ground for the next. This view allows us to look at what level of system is most therapeutic for an addict at any given time, and to assess the individual's capacity to make contact and identify with that level. These levels of system can thus be diagnostic, helping us to describe the addict's present significant boundary relationships.

Understanding an addict client's intrapersonal identity can provide awareness of how he or she interacts with others on a group level. If the client sees him- or herself only as an addict, then he or she will more easily identify with a group of other addicts and have difficulty identifying with the larger world.

The addict is embedded in every one of these systems, like a star in a constellation. The significant issue here for addicts in therapy is their developmental capacity to interact at any of these levels. They may not be aware of themselves as part of these multiple systems. I believe it is useful to perceive one's relationship with others as connected in some way to one's membership in a group or system—such as family, race, country—and at the same time to experience the self as a distinct unit. To first experience "I" is the basis for connection on all of these other levels. Paradoxically, we cannot know "I" without some relationship with others or the environment. We know ourselves in contrast, by our differences and similarities; we know where we end by feeling what we are up against.

In Gestalt therapy, these levels of system are considered to be ongoing or contiguous. The emphasis in therapy is dependent on both the addict's capacity to operate at a particular level and his or her interest or need. For example, the need for affiliation may emphasize the importance of the group level, while growing spiritual interests may bring the addict's focus to the transpersonal level.

In the following chapters, I discuss the addict's experience through the lens of these levels. My underlying belief is that recovery and developmental maturation are synonymous, and that both define the process of moving through and between these levels. We will look at the stages of recovery through these levels of system as the addict's process of expanding and joining the world of others.

Recommended Reading

Adityanee, A., & Murray, R. (1991). The role of genetic predisposition in alcoholism. In I. Glass (Ed.), *The international handbook of addiction behaviour*. London: Tavistock/Routledge.

American Psychiatric Association. (1980). *Diagnostic and Statistical Manual of Mental Disorders*. (3rd ed., revised). Washington, DC: Author.

Brown, S. (1985). *Treating the alcoholic: A developmental model of recovery*. New York: Wiley.

Clemmens, M. (1993). Chemical dependency as a developed contact style. *Gestalt Review, 4* (1), 1–6.

Huckabay, M. (1992). An overview of the theory and practice of Gestalt group therapy. In E. Nevis (Ed.), *Gestalt therapy: Perspectives and applications.* Lake Worth, FL: Gardner Press.

McConville, M. (1995). *Adolescence: Psychotherapy and the emergent self.* San Francisco: Jossey-Bass.

Perls, F. (1969). *Ego, hunger, and aggression.* New York: Vintage Books.

Perls, F., Hefferline, R., & Goodman, P. (1951). *Gestalt therapy: Excitement and growth in the human personality.* New York: Julian Press.

Telfair-Richards, J. (1988). Energy: A Taoist/Gestalt perspective. *Gestalt Review, 3* (1), 1, 8–10.

Valliant, G. (1983). *The natural history of alcoholism.* Cambridge, MA: Harvard University Press.

Wheeler, G. (1991). *Gestalt reconsidered.* Lake Worth, FL: Gardner Press.

White, J. (1995). A special case of Gestalt ethics. *Gestalt Journal, 18* (2), 33–54.

Wilber, K. (1986). *Transformations of consciousness.* Boston: New Science Library.

Zinker, J. (1977). *Creative process in Gestalt therapy.* New York: Brunner/Mazel.

CHAPTER TWO

The Process of Addiction

The Roots of Recovery

M y sense of the relationship between addiction and recovery is that they are two contexts of the same desire for self-survival and meaning. I don't believe that addiction is exclusively night and recovery day, or that addiction is only the disease and recovery the cure. These definitions are simplistic and obscure the possibility that both modes (addiction and recovery) are modes of self-modulation, struggles to adapt the self in an interpersonal field.

In some ways, of course, the analogies I resist can be accurate: as clinicians, we have all seen the apparent rebirth of an alcoholic client who has stopped drinking. We've witnessed the change in personality when a cocaine addict stays clean for ten years. But addiction is more than a digression or an avoidance; it is the search for meaning and survival, one that eventually leads into depths of pain and isolation. Yet those same themes that underlie the addict's search for meaning, so apparent during addiction, reemerge in life and therapy as the client recovers. My vision of this process is of the addict's essential search for meaning as the underground roots that burrow deeply during addiction, only to emerge upward and become the salient themes during recovery. The same roots connect the underground life of addiction with the burgeoning, expanding tree of recovery. Each addict's growth or expansion is influenced not only by the effort to remain abstinent and to change in recovery, but by these roots or themes—themes that shape the addict's experience of self and interpersonal style. In recovery, this shaping is apparent in how recovering addicts make contact, create boundaries with others, and tolerate their own sensations.

THE STAGES OF ADDICTION

To appreciate and work with addicts in recovery, the clinical work is contextualized by the earlier process of addiction that each recovering addict has lived. The process of addiction sets the stage for the tasks and stages of recovery. The following is a short version of the stages of addiction that describe the addict's movement toward an increasingly isolated and self-focused existence, the life of the relationship with the drug. These stages are described as a development of a process and as a form of self-modulation by the addict by which the addict develops the *addiction contact cycle.*

Avoidance

In this first stage of addiction, an awareness such as discomfort when meeting people is modified by taking a drink or drug. In this way, the normal excitement of initial contact is reduced. Each drug has a particular effect on the user, so what is not felt is the excitement of normal life. What is not felt—or is interrupted—is the usual complex of sensations we feel when beginning an experience. This interruption of contact can occur between sensation and awareness so that anxiety or discomfort is never felt or is greatly diminished. This is not the same as the *stimulation* the user derives from drugs such as cocaine and amphetamines. Their effect is a pharmacological one and is experienced by addicts as exciting.

An addict may also drink at the mobilization-action phase so that more chemical use is substituted for talking to or interacting with others. Drinking then serves the additional purpose of "something to do." This can be a large attraction for adolescents, who frequently experience themselves as bored and having nothing to do. Intoxication can provide the stimulation that they may be struggling to develop for themselves and an outlet for increasing energy.

For example, a high school student going to his first dance may discover that the normal fears of being rejected and being observed can be minimized by a few sips of beer. The adolescent then temporarily circumvents the development crisis of socialization by using the drug.

The same process can be used by an adult. A saleswoman under pressure to deliver sales may take to having a drink before meeting customers. As if by magic, the sinking feeling in her stomach goes away and she feels as if she can sell anything. Each sale reinforces her belief and she may even appear self-confident to her customers. Her difficulty occurs when she doesn't have a drink before meeting a customer, because she has relied on liquid confidence and has not developed a sense of her own ability.

In both cases, the potential addict has learned a lesson—certain feelings and awkward experiences can be avoided or even mastered through the use of drugs. If this learning is repeated, both the teenager and the saleswoman will have less tolerance for that same anxiety because they have *a way out.*

Maintenance

At this stage, users attempt to maintain the sense of comfort once achieved through their initial use of alcohol or drugs. This sense of comfort may be within themselves or interpersonally with others (or both). This is the contact modulation or interruption of confluence. Erving and Miriam Polster define *confluence* as "a phantom pursued by people who want to reduce difference so as to moderate the upsetting experience of novelty and otherness." The user of alcohol or drugs has had some success at this by modulating his or her feelings through intoxication. To maintain this, the user will need to more regularly use and eventually increase the dosage. As Perls and his colleagues note, the addict's interpersonal style becomes an attempt to enter "into immediate confluence without preparatory contact with the other person."

An example of this would be the alcoholic who enters a dinner party already intoxicated and talks to newly met people as if they were lifelong friends. At this stage in the process, addicts will use chemicals more and more frequently to re-create such experiences. These falsely warm episodes substitute for relationships rooted in the aware experience of the self and other. Meanwhile, the other guests at the party may barely know this person and not share the addict's sense of a shared good time. Internally, what is maintained is the relaxing or euphoric effects of the drug. The addict seeks to maintain the constant feelings of well-being or confidence produced by the drug.

Diminishing New Figures

After developing some pattern of attempting to maintain this state, the addict has even less tolerance for the energy and excitement of new situations and more desire for familiar, predictable situations. The effect of the drug is the familiar, predictable situation or experience. Alcohol or drugs are used earlier in the contact cycle. The user becomes habituated to warding off the increasing energy of sensation and awareness. Progressively, sensations other than those produced by the drug are experienced as intolerable or "too much." The addict's decreasing tolerance for sensation can be likened to that of a burn victim who, missing an outer layer of skin, experiences the slightest breeze or bump as excruciating pain.

The goal then for the addict's contact style is to not let any new experience emerge by maintaining a familiar *pseudocontact* or *pseudostimulation*. Contact is the spontaneous emergence of a new experience; feelings, thoughts, perceptions are not predicted but are experienced in the relative context of the individual's need and environment. By continuing to influence incoming sensations and experience, the addict creates a familiar recurring experience, a pseudocontact. Paradoxically, the addict experiences each new intoxication or use of the drug as stimulating even though nothing new is experienced. This stimulation does not develop by the natural process of excitement from interaction with others or from the rising energy of self—it is induced by the use of the drug. It is the same old process and thus no new figures emerge. The addict cannot attach any interest to other figures (relationships, professional responsibilities, self-care).

The act of using is now gulping, snorting, or injecting. The drug crosses the contact boundary of self without any discrimination. At this point in the process, using has become introjective; the drink or drug is usually not tasted or experienced at the point of contact.

Narrowing

As the addictive process progresses, the addict's experience becomes narrower, creating what Jesse Carlock refers to as an impoverished ground. The addict has less contact or need for others, less internal sensations, and fewer new ideas. Experience becomes increasingly focused on the addict's own internal world, and less on the world of others as real people. The crisis that mounts now is how to manage growing internal anxiety or discomfort. Once intoxicated, the focus remains on the self and on sustaining the desired experience, restricted and redundant. This narrowed field is what Richard Knowles refers to as a "hopeless" relationship to the world. The addict does not trust nor open the boundary to what is novel or unknown. In a sense, the continuing use of drugs is an attempt to create a predictable and perfect scenario, perhaps a re-creation of that first drunk or perfect glow.

This narrowed world becomes the goal of addiction at this stage, but it becomes increasingly difficult to maintain as the addict's tolerance increases and as life begins to collapse in all directions. Also narrowed is the addict's emotional range. Often addicts at this stage of addiction feel only anger, fear, and the craving for the drug.

Broken Cycles, Broken Promises

By interrupting countless opportunities for completing interactions or contact experiences, the addict creates an enormous backlog of unfinished business. Jobs are lost, marriages dissolved, significant career and relationship opportunities are forgotten or missed. Frequently addicts rationalize or deny the significance of these ruptures and the cause of them (their own drug use) by thinking "I never really liked that job . . . man . . . apartment . . . city . . . anyway." The point of addiction is to avoid unpleasant feeling and sensation, so the mounting shame must be countered by denial and rationalization.

The addict must move away from functional feelings of remorse and longing that may begin to emerge when not intoxicated. By *functional remorse,* I am referring to those feelings that emerge from an awareness of behavior. These feelings are rooted in our connection to others and the reality that if we hit someone with a car when we are drunk, we are responsible for that action. These feelings are the after-effects of the addict's process. The addict resorts, of course, to the surefire method and "drinks to forget." Another emerging sensation is thus interrupted. Drinking or using and then sobering up becomes a perpetual cycle. The addict must avoid the pain of experiencing these feelings and awareness—but each episode of using creates more behavioral problems (auto accidents, arguments, missed appointments) and more negative feelings. Feelings of fear, shame, and remorse grow geometrically.

Eventual Collapse

At this point, the addict's world has narrowed to self and drug, the ultimate "I-it" relationship. Increased tolerance to the substance demands greater consumption. The contact cycle allows the addict to live at almost a minimal level of sensation. Continuing to use, the addict moves physically toward a horizontal position—lying supine, or what is sometimes called "falling down drunk." This is the phenomenon Richard Knowles describes as "horizontality"—a sense of being helpless to the world, unable to emotionally or even physically deal with the environment that looms over and around the addict. Many addicts actually reach this physical position in the later stages of their using, but still others describe themselves as feeling "below people, flattened . . . unable to get up . . . helpless . . . like a child."

This state of existential horizontality—losing the capacity to stand up and engage the world in a contactful manner—is the most critical moment in the progression of addiction. It is a moment of decision that may recur repeatedly for addicts; they may move in and out of this collapsed state for years. The longer addicts stay at this stage, the more difficult it may be for them to imagine a different life, a life without alcohol or drugs. They so fully organize the field around getting, using, and having the drug that there may be little else in their awareness. This is often the experience of skid row alcoholics or long-term narcotics users.

EFFECTS OF THE STAGES

These stages emphasize the addict's process of influencing experience through repeated use of drugs and alcohol. It is a developing process of narrowing focus and almost exclusive interest in the drug. But the effect of the drug creates layers of desensitization that then allow the addict to continue the behavior without second thoughts or remorse. Thus the process is self-perpetuating; the addict uses to feel better or more comfortable—but when intoxicated behaves in ways that when sober produce discomfort. The cure for what ails the addict becomes that which ails him or her. Clearly, there are larger levels of system both involved and collaborative with the addict's use of drugs. No addict is in this process alone. But the initial task in recovery will be for the addict to maintain his or her boundary with drugs, no matter what others do.

It is inaccurate to suggest that all addicts go through these stages at the same pace or intensity—or even that all start at stage one and end at stage six. Many alcoholics begin drinking and then *develop* an intolerance for sensation through years of social drinking. Still other addicts can live at the stage of maintaining confluence for ten or twenty years, similar to E. M. Jellinek's *Delta* alcoholics or methadone users. These addicts appear to stay at a certain stage and show little overt difficulty unless they are forced to stop using. Then they experience withdrawal and the craving as if they had gone through the entire progression of addiction. For recovering addicts, it is the emotional, physiological, and psychological effects of this process that need to be addressed in recovery. Some of these effects can be seen as themes that existed before the addiction process and emerge in recovery.

FUNDAMENTAL THEMES OF ADDICTION AND RECOVERY

As addicts move from addiction and into recovery, fundamental themes form the ground of the addict's field. These themes often exist before addicts begin to use and frequently have their origin in the addict's family or early life patterns of contact. Also, these themes can develop over the progression of the addict's use of drugs—for example, addicts become less trusting during years of using drugs. As mentioned earlier, I think of these themes as roots—processes that work underground during the addict's use of drugs and emerge in a different form in recovery, like runners that spread out beneath a tree and rise to send up new trunks. The shape of the addict's recovery, like a tree, is the product of these roots and the care and attention given to their growth.

Trust

Trust is a fundamental theme for addicts. As Erik Erikson describes, trust of others and inevitably of self is based in the early development experiences of contact with parents and family. As infants are limited in their ability to self-regulate and self-care, they must come to some mode of contact with the significant others in their life. During this period, the infant must engage and be engaged by another in order to develop a sense of self. The infant is literally horizontal in the world, and from this position of vulnerability, develops a basic contact mode with the world. Infants must either learn to trust and engage with others (by relaxing their bodies and accepting environmental support) or engage mostly with self (by tightening and turning their need and focus inward).

This experience becomes a metapattern for the developing person as he or she grows into adolescence and adulthood. When childhood experiences of contact have been generally positive, the person learns to trust (be open) to what is novel and spontaneous. But if one has learned to mistrust others and feel exclusively reliant on self-support, then there is little tolerance for new, spontaneous experiences. The person may be overly self-determined, and actually avoid the experience of relying on others.

One resolution to the addict's conflict of trust is to use drugs. This helps to blur the self-other boundary, diminishes environmental awareness, and maintains only a minimal awareness within the self. A common resolution in recovery is to become overly self-determined, trying to manage self and others.

Shame

Addicts often experience a sense of shame in their interactions. This feeling can exist in addicts for years prior to using drugs, and permeates their experience of approaching the boundary with others. According to Bob Lee, *shame* "is the experience that what is me is not acceptable, that this is not my world." Out of a belief that "what is me" will not be supported or validated by the environment, addicts disown aspects of the self; they may refuse to try, hold back, settle for less, and generally diminish their presence.

I believe the experience of shame develops later in life, when it is possible to act on one's needs. Shaming is based on a separation between self and other; when the other does not know of our need, we must ask or reach. The shame of acting in ways not supported by others leaves us frustrated. Drug use allows addicts to further disown what they perceive as a shameful need or want (part of self) by allowing them not to feel the self as distinctly.

In recovery, addicts are less desensitized, and thus able to feel their needs. The experience of shame occurs more as the recovering addict emerges into greater presence. But the addict may also have internalized the shame that was formerly experienced from others, and may now do to self what others have done. By shaming self, an addict can avoid the potential experience of feeling shamed by others. This is often a theme in therapy with long-term addicts who have criticized or shamed themselves in order to inhibit addictive behaviors.

Furthermore, addicts often feel greater and additional shame for their behavior when intoxicated. This feeling is more than remorse; it is a deeper self-revulsion, a turning inward away from others. The more an addict feels shame about drug use, the more appealing the desensitizing effect of the drug. The problem becomes the solution. Others (including the therapist) may take on the face of the addict's shame by further shaming and criticizing, sometimes under the intention of confrontation or breaking down denial. Often others react to the addict's behavior critically, appearing discomforted or repulsed. It is difficult not to have such reactions when an addict passes out at his three-year-old daughter's birthday party, or clutches a wine bottle as he sits on a city sidewalk, his filthy clothing soaked with urine. Addicts who have felt shame for years react to this environmental response as reinforcement of their basic badness, and as cause for renewed flight from the world.

As an addict continues into recovery, the sense of shame can permeate social interactions. In therapy, this process may appear in the recovering addict's withholding feelings and experiences for fear of being "judged . . . analyzed . . . misunderstood." It is often our task as therapists to help articulate and define these feelings as they exist between ourselves and our recovering addict clients.

Confidence

The sense of confidence or competency develops later in life than trust and shame, but is based upon those two ground structures. The ability to accomplish actions and goals is based on an interpersonal field that is both supportive and validating. When individuals don't trust their environment, they tend to avoid trying new behaviors; this leaves them either lacking in confidence that they are able to do so or arrogantly sure that they can do anything. For anyone who has worked with addicts, this polarity will sound quite familiar. Feeling shame or avoiding shame may thus result in a lack of creative action. Without acting or experimenting, we cannot learn anything new or feel confident that we are capable of learning. The effect is circular; we lack the confidence to act, and without acting, fail to develop a sense of confidence as a ground for action.

Alcohol and other drugs can supply a form of confidence. A client of mine referred to bourbon as "artificial nerve"—one drink and he felt he could do anything. Once high, he was the smartest, handsomest, funniest person at the party. His difficulty occurred when he wasn't drunk and the haunting feelings of shame and incompetence returned. Addicts often appear overly confident to the point of bravura.

This is usually a compensation, an "as if" behavior adopted to mask self-doubt.

In active addiction, many details of daily life can be left unattended or only minimally accomplished. The addict often enters recovery with little experience of accomplishing tasks, and perhaps also with the sense, as one of my clients described, of "trying or setting out to do things but never finishing. I began to wonder whether I could do it anymore."

The therapeutic task with recovering addicts is often to help them reexperience their capacity to interact and follow through. This is one of the changes that occur when the addict moves from the shortened addiction style of sensation-action to the more complete cycle of sensation, awareness, mobilization, contact, assimilation, and withdrawal.

Boredom

In experiencing the self and interacting with others, a certain amount of excitement naturally builds and peaks: this is the process described in Chapter One. This developing excitement occurs in a wave, with minimal excitement at the beginning of the experience, rising excitement as one moves toward the encounter, and diminishing excitement as one withdraws from the experience. Addicts have difficulty tolerating either the lower amount of excitement at the end of the process or the intensity of too much at the beginning and middle. The former is often experienced as boredom, and is a cause for using drugs; the latter is experienced as intolerable, and is a cause for using drugs.

The experience of boredom is thus another aspect of ground that can be temporarily resolved through drug use. An example is Carlton, a seventy-five-year-old alcoholic who began drinking upon retirement. He was faced with the potential boredom of a less active life, and began drinking cocktails while golfing with friends. Carlton soon graduated to daily drinking when he discovered that drinking was not boring. His drinking pattern occurred in the later period of life, when he wanted to avoid suffering the lack of stimulation he feared from retirement. The developmental issue of finding meaning and fulfillment when not working became the background or context for his drinking.

Boredom is an intolerance for lower levels of stimulation, or for the Yin energy of closure and precontact. This intolerance occurs in certain children and often in adolescents. "If it's not fast, startling, or different," a teenage client of mine would say, "then what good is it?" Being bored is based on an expectation that the environment will entertain or stimulate us. Alcohol and many kinds of drugs can supply the entertainment and stimulation that some individuals don't know or don't expect to develop in themselves. It is the ultimate arrogance, the expectation that the world or an other should "do me . . . make me feel different."

—⁓—

These themes form the basis for the addict's experience of life, both when using and in recovery. They are what Wheeler calls *ground structures,* feelings and beliefs that shape the addict's experience of events. They may be so embedded in the addict's field that they remain unarticulated; the addict client may not have words for these fundamental themes. It is the therapist's task to help the client experience, articulate, and work through these themes.

The following chapters give numerous examples of these themes in the lives of recovering addicts as well as examples of working through them in therapy. Active use of drugs for addicts is a means of modulating these experiences. The approach I describe provides an alternative to the addict's pattern of either avoiding or exclusively tolerating these experiences. The roots of recovery are a new pattern of coping with these experiences.

Recommended Readings

Carlock, C., Glaus, K., & Shaw, C. (1992). The alcoholic: A Gestalt view. In E. Nevis (Ed.), *Gestalt therapy: Perspectives and applications.* Lake Worth, FL: Gardner Press.

Erikson, E. (1963). *Childhood and society.* New York: Norton.

Jellinek, E. (1960). *The disease concept of alcoholism.* New Haven, CT: College and Universities Press.

Knowles, R. (1986). *Human development and human possibility.* Lanham, MD: University Press.

Perls, F., Hefferline, R., & Goodman, P. (1951). *Gestalt therapy: Excitement and growth in the human personality.* New York: Julian Press.

Polster, E., & Polster, M. (1973). *Gestalt therapy integrated.* New York: Brunner/Mazel.

Wheeler, G. (1991). *Gestalt reconsidered.* Lake Worth, FL: Gardner Press.

CHAPTER THREE

The Challenge of Recovering Addicts as Clients

—᷒ᜰᜰ᷒— Therapy with recovering addicts can be quite different from intervening with addicts who are actively using. As addicts develop and change in recovery, their interpersonal fields become more complex and varied. Often the recovering client has focused consistently on not using drugs but is stuck in some other process. We meet recovering clients who chronically repeat old patterns, who are difficult to work with for a variety of reasons, and who view therapy as a threat or as competition with their other support systems such as Alcoholics Anonymous and Narcotics Anonymous.

The longer an addict's period of recovery, the greater the need to focus in therapy on problems of social integration and questions of existential meaning. Other common issues that emerge in therapy with recovering addicts are personality disorders, relapse, and unfinished business from addiction or early recovery. In this chapter, I provide examples of some such cases. These are all "after sobriety" clients who have worked in therapy either with me or with other clinicians. I present them here as examples of the kinds of clients with whom many of us struggle, and whom we may consider failures or hard cases.

THE PASSIVE CLIENT

These first two cases are examples of confluent clients: clients who don't define their needs or take responsibility for the therapy process. The first client for the most part goes along with the therapy process, but doesn't progress. The second is confluent in the sense that he is cooperating with some external direction and doesn't define what he wants or who he is in relation to the therapist. In both situations, the therapist runs the risk of working on an apparently passive client.

EDWARD

Edward came to therapy when referred by his lover, a recovering addict. He had been abstinent for over twenty years without attending AA or any support group. In fact, Edward had never been to therapy since he had stopped using. Despite his lack of involvement in twelve step programs, Edward had changed his lifestyle and was very involved in the community. He had been married twice and divorced within a few years. Although he generally seemed friendly and kind, Edward had a quick temper, and often experienced a physical symptom of severe pains in the neck.

My experience of working with Edward was like walking though molasses. He was cooperative but we never got anywhere. Each time either of us felt some sense of closure on significant themes, such as anger or loneliness, he would revert to the old pattern of behavior. I suggested that he might try some twelve step meetings as a support, but he refused. He would listen to me and cooperate but would not make any significant changes. I suggested that he tell me what he didn't like about therapy or what would be helpful to him. He replied that my idea was helpful.

Edward remarried and he and his new wife began couples therapy with me soon after. He was frequently jealous and angry, although she seemed committed to him. The couples therapy was somewhat successful in that their fighting decreased and he became more trusting. Soon after, he terminated therapy "due to finances." I asked them to come in for a closure session, and they of course did.

I heard again from Edward. He wrote me a long letter, telling me he was using drugs after twenty five years, was being treated by a psychiatrist, and was in the process of another divorce. He wanted to return to therapy and attended two sessions, canceling the third without explanation. Edward was not a difficult client during the session, but his lack of substantial change and his ongoing unhappiness make him a common example of an addict who stays mired in old patterns of withdrawal.

ALLEN

Allen had been recovering for fifteen years when he began to feel "lost." He talked about this many times at AA meetings, was given feedback and suggestions from other members, but nothing seemed to satisfy him. One of the suggestions given him was to begin therapy.

Allen came to therapy saying, "My sponsor told me to come, and I follow his directions." Although Allen was in deep pain and had questions about his life's directions, he remained focused on therapy as a task he was doing because "it's good for me." The therapist tried approaches to draw her client out, but Allen remained with his pattern of following directions. They met for a number of sessions, until Allen terminated because he was "not getting anything out of this stuff." Despite the therapist's efforts to get him to take some responsibility for the process, Allen continued to view therapy as something he showed up for, something that had been prescribed as good for him.

I consulted with Allen's therapist on a weekly basis. She and I discussed Allen's progress and her growing frustration. It was as if Allen was waiting for her to do something to him while he merely presented himself. She decided she would go back to Allen and share this interpretation with him. When she did, Allen listened and then said, "Well, if that's all you have to say . . . then I don't think you can help me." Allen left angry and did not return for any future sessions.

In working with these clients, both therapists were attempting to *treat* the client. This passive relationship, one in which the client presents himself to be worked on, is not an uncommon one among recovering addicts. The model out of which the client often operates is that of a student addressing a mentor. Edward and Allen maintained themselves in an undifferentiated pattern as a way of coping with their addiction and strong feelings. It is only when clients like these can risk showing differences with their therapist, and risk experiencing their own feelings, that any change can occur. Equally, it is only when the therapist is willing to get out of the role of expert or mentor that any therapeutic change can occur.

WHAT'S THE USE?

The following two stories are examples of clients who reach a point in their recovery where they wonder if there is any use to their life or relationship. These clients are often referred immediately for some kind of psychiatric evaluation. While that may be necessary, what these examples illustrate is the effect of a kind of frozen development in recovery and the resulting feeling of hopelessness.

ELLEN

Ellen came to therapy because of the way she felt after sixteen years of recovery in AA. At the early part of her recovery, she felt excited about the changes she was experiencing. It was like "going from a black and white TV to a big screen color set." But through the years, she felt increasingly bored and unexcited by her weekly grind of attending meetings. She told me she felt like she just was going through the motions of life. Ellen had been prescribed an antidepressant by her family physician. My sense of Ellen was that she had stopped growing in any direction of interest to her. She had become accustomed to living a life of maintenance: just staying sober had become the focus of her existence.

Ellen's experience in therapy was extensive. She consulted many therapists, each of whom took a different approach; however, she didn't stay with any therapist for more than a few sessions. She also didn't experience much improvement from antidepressants. I believe this is because Ellen was not truly depressed, just frozen in her process of recovery. She had never developed a meaning in her life beyond her abstinence. She was bitter, sarcastic, and unhappy. All that was missing was the drink. But Ellen did not drink; she remains abstinent to this day and continues to shop for therapists. It's clear that she is searching for something but that she's uncertain what this "something" is, and therapy thus continues to feel to her like a useless exercise.

When I tried to suggest to Ellen that she might have to attend to unfinished work in therapy, she was not pleased. She wanted me to fix "it." I expressed to her that she had been given many alternatives, both therapists and medication. I believed that if she wanted to do more than go through the motions of life, *she* would have to make changes—not change therapists. Ellen decided that this was the same "useless" advice she had been given to her by previous therapists and her AA sponsor. She ended therapy with me on that note. I had decided to be direct with Ellen rather than offer one more promise of cure.

MARY AND STEVE

Mary and Steve had been married for ten years. They met in a twelve step program, attending meetings together for two years before they ever dated. By the time they called me for an appointment, Mary and Steve had been sober for almost fifteen years. My initial reaction to them was that they were friendly people, a little detached from their feelings. As I listened to them interact, it was clear that they spoke to each other in a kind of shared reference of twelve step language. When I asked them why they had come to therapy, Mary said that they didn't know how to talk to each other anymore. Steve felt there was nothing left in their marriage. As a couple, they were in a common stage after seven to ten years of marriage: they'd reached a sense of distance and disconnection from the bonding that often occurs earlier in marriage.

I asked Mary and Steve what they had in common. Besides their children, they felt they had little in common except the "program." I asked them to talk to each other so that I could get a sense of how they interacted. As I listened and watched them, I was struck by the same sense of flatness they'd complained to me of. Their interactions were stale and usually in the form of one partner's sharing his or her thoughts: "I wonder what's the use . . . it's a question of putting first things first . . . I know when I'm angry with you it's my disease talking." Often these statements were punctuated with self-analysis and twelve step jargon. My image of them was of two people sitting in a room together, each managing by analyzing his or her own thoughts, wrapping up personal experience in thought-balloons. There was little spontaneity in their conversation and their way of being with each other.

Mary and Steve talked to one another as if they were at a twelve step discussion meeting. In fact, this was the manner in which they had always connected, but now it offered them little richness in their relationship. In the following sessions, both partners disclosed that they had gone outside the marriage for excitement. Neither of these affairs had been significant, but rather, attempts to feel good and alive. Mary and Steve were a difficult couple to work with because I had to teach them how to talk *to* each other in emotional language rather than about themselves.

What made this work so hard was how entrenched Mary and Steve had become in their identities as addicts, to the exclusion of seeing themselves as a couple. Another difficulty was all the pent-up feelings that emerged once they began to express themselves, as they had created a pattern of interaction that prevented them from experiencing these feelings. The process of learning to articulate emotions took months, as they expressed and dealt with years of loneliness, hurt, and anger.

Mary and Steve are typical of many long-term recovering addicts, people who have become experts at attending to their own boundaries and thereby preventing the development and enrichment of their relationships. The challenge for me as their therapist was to help them develop a mutual boundary that allowed them to express their feelings and join together.

AM I REALLY AN ADDICT?

One of the most common challenges we face is that of clients who return to drug use after some period of abstinence. We might diagnose these clients as relapsing, but what if the client no longer believes he or she is an addict or alcoholic? This client is an example of someone who entered therapy after some period of abstinence.

DEBBIE'S SLIDE

In her eight years of recovery, Debbie developed an excellent professional reputation as an attorney. She had a booming practice, drove a Jaguar, and dated many attractive men. She often wondered why she continued to feel as if she were sick and different from normal people. In the first years of her sobriety, Debbie remembered the pain and fear of her cocaine addiction. But after five years of attending meetings, Debbie began to drop off her involvement in Narcotics Anonymous to one meeting per week. When Debbie entered therapy, she had dropped back to one meeting per month, "for social reasons." The therapist Debbie worked with was impressed by how well Debbie had done in her recovery.

Most of the work they did in therapy focused on helping Debbie realize her potential. The primary emphasis of this work was on Debbie herself, with little attention paid to how she interacted with others, including the therapist. Debbie began to meditate daily and to attend workshops focused on contacting "your inner guide." When the therapist suggested that Debbie join a therapy group, Debbie responded that she would "try" if her schedule permitted. After a few more sessions, Debbie terminated therapy, thanking her therapist for helping her grow so fully.

Three months later, Debbie called me for an appointment. She came to the session well dressed and looking calm. The first thing she said was that she used to think she was an addict but that she'd recently begun to "have a glass of wine" with dinner. When I asked her why, Debbie said she was tired of seeing other people have fun, and of feeling as if she were "not normal."

The challenge of working with Debbie was the question of whether she really was an addict. Her statement that she "used to think she was an addict" flies in the face of what many therapists believe: that addicts can never learn to drink or use again. Yet the working place for therapy needs to be the client's experience. While I believed that Debbie probably was an addict and would not be able to drink without returning to the addiction cycle, I needed to begin with Debbie's desire to see herself as normal and not an addict. This can often be the challenge in working with relapsed addicts. They may not be addicted, even though they once believed they were. The other possibility is that this person is an addict and is rationalizing the return to drugs.

In Debbie's case, she was an addict. The work that I did with her was twofold. I worked with her in therapy to explore her desire to be normal and feelings of being different. And second, to address her belief that she could drink, I suggested that she try drinking and notice what happened. She did this for about two months. At the end of that time, she entered a session and informed me that she had been arrested for driving while intoxicated. I asked her what she thought of this occurrence. Debbie said: "I can't control alcohol either." We spent many sessions working through Debbie's anger that she couldn't, as well as exploring her definition of normal. The approach I took with Debbie was very different from the one I would have taken when I first worked as a therapist. Then I would have confronted her about her denial of her addiction and probably gotten her to comply with me or end therapy. Now I knew that I could not control her behavior and believed that if she did some research on her drug use, she could find out for herself if she was an addict.

THE QUESTION OF MEDICATION

Peter made an emergency appointment with one of my colleagues. After twelve years of sobriety, he was clearly in distress. As she talked to him, he sounded depersonalized and frightened. Peter came in for a session the following morning, accompanied by his teenage son. The therapist diagnosed quickly that Peter was experiencing some kind of psychotic episode. He had been thinking about drinking to "calm myself down" but knew that wasn't an answer.

Peter's therapist recommended that he get an immediate psychiatric evaluation. When she suggested this, Peter became more agitated. "I can't do drugs or I'll be back in my addiction . . . If I was going to do that, I wouldn't be here with you." The therapist found herself in a quandary. She knew that therapy alone would not help Peter through his immediate episode, yet Peter viewed the use of medication as a breach of his sobriety. During recovery, Peter had refused to cross his boundary with any mood-altering drug; he had never had surgery and had refused pain medication during oral surgery.

Many of us who work with recovering addicts have encountered this fear of medication. The easy answers are overly simplistic: the difference between getting high and taking medication is that the latter is physician prescribed and it is necessary, versus the counter that a drug is a drug is a drug. Many of us have been faced with this impasse. The harder answers relate to recovering addict-clients' beliefs about their own boundary with drugs. Peter eventually agreed to a short-term hospitalization at a facility for recovering addicts with secondary or dual diagnosis. There he was given support for needing both to stay abstinent and to receive treatment by medication. Such a choice is often very difficult for recovering addicts, who sometimes feel they are copping out by taking medication, or even by trying psychotherapy. For the recovering addict and therapist, this can raise the question, What is sobriety? I believe that, like Peter, some recovering addicts need medication for psychological processes. But I also have seen many addicts abuse prescribed medication. As a profession, we are not responsible for this kind of outcome, but need to attend to the recovering addict's abstinence as well as their other psychological processes.

—◦◦◦—

These cases are examples of some of the challenges we face in working with recovering addicts in therapy. The questions of clients' active involvement in the therapy process, additional psychological processes, and loss of hope occur frequently in my practice. Patterns of contact such as those I've described in Mary and Steve are very common among recovering addicts. Questions I am often faced with in working with these clients is how do I understand the addicts' struggle in terms of their own growth and what are the necessary tasks to move through these struggles? In the next chapter, I outline the stages and tasks of recovery that can serve as guidelines for working with cases like these.

CHAPTER FOUR

The Developmental Stages and Tasks of Recovery

T his chapter describes the processes of recovery through the lens of self-modulation as presented in Chapter One. Stages of recovery are defined by specific tasks for addicts, possible interventions by therapists, and clinical examples. This will provide the framework for case examples of long-term recovery, and for discussion of successful long-term recovery as well as relapse.

The addict has ended up living through abbreviated and intense contact experiences, and so we can see recovery as a process of returning to more complete cycles of contact. In the long term, we can see recovery from the addiction contact style as *the progressive restoration of contact functioning*. The addict has been modulating his or her behavior, and will need to develop or relearn certain contact skills. In the development of a new contact style, these skills will help the addict both to avoid using drugs again and to move into a fuller relationship with the self and others. These fuller relationships are the result of recovering addicts' developing the capacity to sustain their experience beyond habitual stopping points of discomfort.

These stages are developmental rather than temporal. A recovering addict of ten years is not necessarily in third-stage recovery. Some addicts can spend twenty years at stage one, simply maintaining their abstinence. Still others move to later-stage recovery tasks in five years. But like traditional psychological development, some issues or conflicts and their related tasks become more salient as addicts recover for ten, fifteen, and twenty years.

Obviously, there exist individual differences in the duration and importance of each stage; addicts vary in personality development and environmental contexts. Moreover, these stages are not incremental but can be thought of as points on a spiral that the addict may move through a number of times.

In our work with recovering addicts, we see people living narrowed or restricted lives. Recovery offers the possibility of expansion outward from the self toward others, and beyond the self and others. Each stage of recovery becomes the ground or basis for the next stage. For example, an addict needs to develop the ability to attend to self so as to interact and attend to others. Or to frame it in terms of personality development, one needs to *have* a self in order to *be* a self with others. Another example is the capacity for interpersonal contact as the basis for interacting on a larger level of system, even a transpersonal level. Paradoxically, the addict does not develop a self in isolation but in relation to others, a self that emerges from that relationship. The larger system serves as a boundary for addicts, helping to define and provide context to the recovering self. For example, addicts who have not learned how to attend to self and their own boundary will tend to fuse in interpersonal interactions or feel lost in groups or systems.

Based on these observations, I have organized the stages of recovery according to developmental issues, with related tasks supporting development within each stage. To summarize the stages:

Stages of Recovery

STAGE	FOCUS	TASKS
Early Recovery (development of boundaries)	*Self*	Maintaining abstinence Developing retroflection Developing sensations into awareness
Middle Recovery (relatedness and differentiation)	*Self and others*	Complementarity Boundary flexibility and redefinition Interpersonal competence Cooperation

STAGE	FOCUS	TASKS
Later Recovery (expanding self)	*Beyond self and others*	Reflection and contemplation Transcendence

STAGE 1—EARLY RECOVERY: DEVELOPMENT OF SELF AND SELF-BOUNDARIES

The recovering addict's struggle in early recovery is focused on learning to "bound out" drugs and alcohol and to become increasingly sensitized to self. Because of this focus, many of our therapeutic interventions will concentrate on the addicts themselves, their own self-awareness, how they think or dialogue internally, how they acquire self-inhibitions (retroflection). This stage is a transitional one; if it becomes permanent, the recovering addict remains in a kind of extended narcissism, where the self *is* the world and others are not important.

The interventions I describe are based on the self-modulation model of addiction and the recovery process of moving from the addiction cycle to the fuller cycle of experience. The first two tasks center on making that change with drugs and alcohol. The remainder of the tasks of recovery take this process of fuller contact beyond the self and beyond sobriety.

Task: Abstinence as Self-Regulation

Organismic self-regulation is one of the useful concepts in Gestalt therapy. Each individual is regarded as an organism regulating its own intake, managing its boundaries and energy in a self-preserving manner. Eventually, the addict cannot self-regulate while intoxicated, nor can a true addict regulate the drug or drink as a normal drinker does. This is the essence of addiction. As many of us have experienced in our work with addicts in early recovery, it is not useful to exhort an addict to use willpower because anyone's will is subject to limitations, including those chemically induced. It is also pointless for addicts to investigate their reasons for using while intoxicated. The reasons or functions that drug use serves are issues to be examined after the addict is abstinent.

To achieve abstinence, the addict may initially have to enter a drug-free environment, such as a detoxification unit or rehabilitation center. The old adage, "You can't get drunk without a drink!" is a useful maxim for this stage of bounding. The addict needs to withdraw from the cycle of addiction (see Figure 1.2) before he or she can begin a new cycle.

Withdrawal from drugs is often an emotionally and physically painful experience, and it is this pain and discomfort that the addict needs to integrate. Many of the feelings and sensations the addict has avoided through chronic intoxication now rush back in a virtual flood. The addict often feels desperate, and the desire for drugs to desensitize the pain becomes intense.

The first task of recovery is for the addict to self-regulate by becoming abstinent and keeping the drug out of the body. While this seems like common sense, many therapists continue to attempt to teach alcoholics controlled drinking. I have had no clinical or personal experience whatsoever of alcoholics or addicts who learn to control their drug use. I have worked with some individuals who abused drugs and alcohol at one time in life and later returned to controlled, nonproblematic use of drugs—but I believe that those individuals were not addicted. In my opinion, controlled drinking may be possible—but if we are to really study this, we must follow individuals for years, not for a few weeks or in laboratory settings.

It is the paradox of recovery that the addict acknowledges the limitation of not being able to control alcohol and drugs and yet regains control over life; to have the experience of personal will as useless when drinking yet needing to exert will to not drink. This task is a process of gaining some control by not trying to control. In recognizing powerlessness, the addict becomes empowered. The only criterion for this is not using the drug. In a sense, the addict must learn to trust something other than the desire to drink or use. This is an early level of the later task of transcending the self.

For example, Tim was a regular client for three months before he told me he had a drinking problem. When he said he was worried about not being able to stop drinking, I suggested that he experiment with trying to moderate his drinking for a few days. He returned the following week and reported that he had not been able to do this for even one day. He felt that he should be able to manage his drinking, but had ended up drunk five of the seven days between our sessions. He wanted to not drink.

I suggested to Tim that he might need external support in accomplishing this goal, a supportive environment in which alcohol would not be immediately available, a kind of "external boundary." After attending some AA meetings, this became Tim's metaphor for abstinence: something beyond himself, like a perimeter or an extra fence. The perimeter that he created was to attend meetings, to live with his brother (who didn't drink), and to continue in therapy sessions. In all these contexts, he continued to talk about his desire to use—but he has not done so. As I write, Tim has been abstinent for three years.

My major intervention with Tim at this point was to help him see his craving as the result of habituation, and as the potential beginning of a new cycle of using. He needed external support to remain in the struggle of withdrawal, to help inhibit his desire to use again. External support and education of addiction as a process can help interrupt the highly charged beginning of the addiction cycle. The therapeutic work here is to remain focused on the addict's withdrawal, to understand his craving as part of, as well as an avoidance of, the withdrawal process. My way of working with Tim's initial concern about his drinking was to have him try to drink in moderation. My intention was to have him collect more data, to test for himself whether he could moderate his own drinking, rather than for me to tell him he was an alcoholic. I have found in some cases that the latter move can be useful, but most clients, like Tim, need to experiment with controlling their drinking so they can determine for themselves that they cannot.

Task: Learning to Retroflect

The second skill addicts need to develop or reacquire is the ability to inhibit their desire for the drug. *Retroflection,* as defined by Perls, Hefferline, and Goodman, is the turning back toward the self of that which is intended for something outside self. The addict has habitually reached for the drug or drink. Retroflecting, for the addict, is the process of pulling an arm back from the drug or drink, or of stopping any action toward using drugs or alcohol. It is a counter-movement or inhibition, and may include a consideration (awareness) of what using drugs would mean. Initially, then, retroflecting is a conscious inhibition of an habituated pattern, one that will allow addicts to more fully experience themselves, and specifically to experience feelings they have desensitized through years of drug use. It will also develop a richer ground and interests other than the drug.

For addicts, learning to inhibit the desire to drink, as well as other impulses, not only is crucial to recovery but is a major change in their way of interacting. Retroflection clearly interrupts the pattern, discussed earlier, of the addict's moving from sensation to action. Inhibiting the sensation-action pattern both stops the addict from getting high and allows the emergence of fuller sensations that can be experienced and identified, thus allowing the individual to develop a broader palette of feelings and sensations.

Another retroflection that addicts need to learn is *self-talk,* or "thinking before drinking." This involves thinking through the desire for the drug to remember the eventual and inevitable consequences that have occurred before. In early recovery, the addict is not often adept at this kind of thinking, and so the figure of the drug remains in the foreground. Talking to someone else (often another recovering addict) before taking a drug or drink can be a means of developing alternative thoughts and even alternative figures (such as hunger, fatigue, loneliness). The therapist can interact with the client in this pattern, and the client can be directed to discuss with the therapist the urge to use drugs. But my experience is that the more supports an addict has to sound out a craving, the less likely that addict is to actually use.

This dialogue with others can support the addict in two ways. First, addicts can internalize the other person's statements to draw on at other times, and can begin to self-talk in the same way, thereby building an inhibition. Second, this process is an interpersonal one that involves the addict's moving from the intrapersonal level of system (exclusively with self) to collaboration with others. This contact provides support for the addict to stay with the discomfort of an immediate experience by working on that discomfort within a relationship.

Another intervention that can be useful is for the therapist to help the client think through the consequences of using drugs. It is an *extremely normal* behavior for an addict to think of using. The actual consequences and resulting feelings of using drugs are what the addict usually doesn't think about, and what therefore needs to be brought into the addict's awareness. It is usually necessary initially for the therapist to carry this awareness. Particularly helpful is for the therapist to ask the client, "What would happen if you drank?"

I remember working with Tom, a chronic IV heroin user who had been clean for six months and was thinking about "one good last high." His arms were itching, ready for a shot. Despite feeling so much "better than I had in years," Tom wanted to use heroin, and had even gone so far as to locate where he could buy it. I suggested that he take me through the entire experience *after* he used. He went through this in detail with much repeated encouragement from me of "And then what happened?" until he got to his imagined arrest and his awareness that he had just shared a needle with an HIV-infected user. His face turned ashen and his whole body began to settle into the chair as he said, "I thought I was done with this shit!"

This process was intended to walk Tom through his action as fantasy, while emphasizing the full experience as a retroflective technique. He repeatedly used this self-awareness in the months following this session, and reported that by following through without action, he was able to remember many of the most painful and frightening events in his active addiction. An essential piece of this experiment was to emphasize Tom's experience *after* using, the second half of the contact cycle. When addicts crave drugs, they think only of their present discomfort and the rush of the initial high.

Task: Developing Sensations into Awareness

Retroflecting is a skill that allows addicts in early recovery to inhibit their desire to use, and in later recovery, to transcend their impulsive pattern of acting without awareness. It allows them time to address the question, "What am I responding to with this action?" The next step in the recovery process is for addicts to develop the sensations they have habitually avoided into clear feelings they can experience, articulate, and understand. This cultivation of feelings opens the recovering addict to a richer life, but that is not necessarily an immediate advantage. Ironically, the very reason the addict either entered into or maintained a pattern of drug use and consequent desensitization was to *avoid* experiencing certain feelings, to *avoid* becoming fully aware of self and others. To develop their sensations more fully, recovering addicts have to both cultivate new patterns of behavior—along with the skills to support those patterns—and allow themselves to experience (feel, think, sense) some of what they have structured their whole lives to avoid.

I am thinking of Arnold, a client who frequently came to sessions wanting to use drugs. We had processed this desire repeatedly, and each time he left the session without the desire. He came to a session one day and began again talking about how he'd been wanting to get high. I asked him what else he would do or feel if he didn't think about using drugs. After a long period of silence, he said "Sad and angry!" From this awareness, Arnold was able to lean into his sadness and anger. The focus of his work shifted from not using drugs to exploring the feelings and awareness he was not letting emerge.

Arnold's awareness was dependent on his ability to slow down his energy. He did this by developing ways to relax. The therapist may have to teach these relaxation skills to the recovering client. It is important to recognize that the struggle for the addict is not only a cognitive and meaning-making process but an energetic remodulation. As we discussed earlier, addicts tend to become stimulated quickly. Attending to physical groundedness (concrete sensation, that is, having clients attend to feeling their feet on the ground, their back in the chair) can also help to slow them down and anchor them in the moment, which will in turn enable them to tolerate the rising energy of contact resulting in more defined feelings and awareness.

This task of developing sensations into awareness will be a building block for long-term recovery. The addict can now experience self and others, rather than react to or avoid that experience. Through this attention to feelings, the client can find fuller meaning in life experience.

Another example of the need for developing sensations into awareness is recovering addicts' tendency to talk about their experience rather than to feel it. This is part of the addict's pattern of desensitization that is augmented by drug use and that continues long into recovery. An example of this linguistic desensitization is frequent use of terms such as *it* and *the problem* or *the disease,* which allow addicts to keep an emotional distance from their own behavior.

I remember working with Jim, a client who had recently lost his brother to cancer, yet who spoke about this loss as if he were observing an event. In the therapy sessions he would punctuate his statements with "but that's the way it is." He said he learned this statement early in his recovery as a form of acceptance. I was curious about this pattern, since he never seemed to experience his feelings, but rather to move immediately to this remote acceptance. In attempting to help him develop sensation, I asked him to try making sentences that began with "I accept." He agreed to do this and started: "I accept . . . my brother's death . . . the way he died . . . the look on his wife and children's faces at the funeral." As he made these statements, his breathing became shallow and a single tear dropped from his eye. I asked him what he was experiencing. He said he felt sad and angry. So the statement that would have been more accurate was, "I accept my brother's death but I don't like it!" For Jim, feeling his connection to his brother was the next step in recovery. He had developed a pattern of self-management where he "accepted it" in order to stay sober and to avoid becoming overwhelmed by feelings. But at this point in his recovery (ten years) he could feel complex and seemingly contradictory feelings and still "accept."

The conversation with Jim illustrates an intervention that I often use with recovering addicts who have learned to talk about experience instead of living it. One of the indications of this pattern is that the client will show little change in affect, will sound monotonous, or will tend to exclusively observe or sum up personal experience with some cliché. The technique I used here was to have the client experiment with speaking in the first person and notice what he felt as a result. This principle of ownership of experience is fundamental to the Gestalt approach, and serves as the method to accomplish the task of developing sensations.

STAGE 2—MIDDLE RECOVERY: RELATEDNESS AND DIFFERENTIATION

In the middle stage of recovery, recovering addicts begin to move beyond the exclusive focus on self-boundary and sobriety and to include others in their field of awareness. The tasks of this stage are steps toward increased awareness and involvement of interrelatedness. The boundary that the recovering addict experiences is the self-other boundary. Within the stage there is a movement between what Gregory Bateson refers to as *complementarity*, or what Perls, Hefferline, and Goodman refer to as *identification* and *interpersonal differentiation*. This dialectic movement of what is "I" and "not I" is the fundamental process of boundary definition. As the addict moves into this stage of recovery, he or she becomes increasingly aware of being embedded in an interpersonal field, and the task is how to manage and define self in this field.

Because these stages are not chronological, some addicts never move beyond the interpersonal level. The issues they bring to therapy are often based on feeling stuck at this stage, or needing to develop skills to accomplish the related tasks.

Task: Complementarity

According to Bateson, the alcoholic needs to develop a complementary rather than a competitive relationship with the world. This is a crucial but transitory process. This complementarity or confluence is accomplished by *introjecting:* a process of taking in from others with minimal discrimination, a kind of unaware internalization. I earlier described confluence as the experience of "no difference," but want to shift that definition here. Confluence for the early recovering addict can be described as the experience of consistent similarity. The task at this stage for addicts is to experience how they are similar to other addicts. This supports them as they clearly identify the process of addiction and recovery, and develop a support system. Introjection from this perspective is what McConville calls "introjecting the ground." It is an implicit absorption of aspects of the field. In adolescence and other transitional periods of life, what is absorbed are role models, examples of what it is to be an adult: a woman, a man, a recovering addict. In recovery, what is absorbed are possible models of recovery, examples of how to live without alcohol or drugs.

Addicts are already introjectors par excellence, and therapists sometimes become concerned about the tendency in twelve step programs for recovering addicts to use jargon or to speak in terms of "we." For many addicts, it is essential to relax boundaries and absorb from their environment. The language that is initially appropriated provides a cognitive support or framework. Initially, the addict may have to borrow language from authors or other recovering addicts (phrases like "disease model," slogans from AA or NA) to develop a framework for understanding experience and to establish some connection with others. It is crucial for clinicians to see that addicts in the end of their addiction are totally isolated from others. Following from this isolation, a tendency to overidentify or take in without discrimination is often an important step for recovering addicts.

A colleague of mine tells the story of Franklin, a recovering client who seemed incapable of taking feedback from others without interrupting them. He was going to "stay sober" no matter what anyone said or did. This stance was no different from his pattern when using drugs—only the content of what he was saying was different. His process remained one of isolation and an impoverished life, based exclusively on self-reliance.

My colleague asked Franklin his objection to input from others. Franklin snapped back that he had no objection to hearing from others, it was just that he knew what he needed to do. Eventually, he said that he didn't want to be controlled by others. The work of therapy became helping Franklin experience how he could take observations, feelings, and ideas from others without being controlled. He learned to consider what people said to him as possible hypotheses that he might accept or reject. His phrase for this skill was to "sample" what others had to offer, neither swallowing completely nor rejecting without consideration. Like many addicts, Franklin defined himself in terms of his differences from others, in this case to the extent that he viewed external influence as a danger to his integrity.

As recovery progresses and as addicts distance themselves from the act of using and develop some interrelatedness, the necessity to learn from others must be balanced with the need to differentiate. Recovering addicts develop their own sense of recovery and their own language. The problem with maintaining an introjective style indefinitely is that recovering addicts may become disgusted and reject not only what isn't theirs, but their entire recovery as well. Out of the need for differentiation, the recovering addict may use again. Many active addicts continue to parrot the words of others while using. Other addicts may attempt to remain in confluence with others and thus postpone their inevitable differentiation. To maintain this confluence, they must retroflect their own potentially differentiating thoughts, words, or actions. Continuing to retroflect eventually builds up frustration, fatigue, and resentment, feelings that may be experienced by addicts as an impetus to use drugs.

Larry is an example of a client who struggled with this middle process. He attended NA meetings regularly for two years, and his experience was one of gaining practical support for living a clean life. Larry developed some malfunction in his heart, and was prescribed medication to modify the irregularity. When he talked about his condition at meetings, he was accused of getting high by some members of the group. This presented a significant conflict for Larry, who did "everything they told me to do at meetings." His initial response to this confrontation was to feel that he had done something wrong. Because of his shame and guilt, Larry was prepared to stop taking the medication (which had no intoxicating effects).

In our session, Larry described himself as feeling torn between his own health and his loyalty to the twelve step group. I asked Larry if he thought he was high. He answered "No! I don't feel high . . . I don't want to get high." I responded that he could pay attention to what he had just said.

The task for Larry was to discriminate his own experience from what others believed. This was a change for Larry, who had just spent two years learning not to trust his immediate experience, especially in regard to drugs. As Larry's therapist, I chose to challenge the accusation that Larry had internalized, so he could examine his own experience that he was not high. This was also an important developmental step in recovery for Larry: to attend to his own experience even if he disagreed with others in the twelve step program. Larry mistrusted his own process so much that he nearly threatened his life based on what someone else believed. After talking with his NA sponsor and with me in therapy, Larry was able to differentiate from the accusations and attend to *his own experience.*

The other possible conflict is that of a recovering client who is actually on the verge of using again. I remember a client of mine named Paul who had surgery, and who—long after the actual procedure—revealed to me that he had hoarded the pain medication for "when things got bad." His friends had noticed his behavior as different after the surgery, and they confronted him. Paul became angry with them; when he did the same with me in therapy, I focused on his competitive or adversarial tone. I told him that it seemed to me that he must have something at stake to fight so hard, and that's when he revealed to me that he had hidden the drugs.

One difference between these two clients is that while Larry was already considering what others had said to him, Paul was not. He was not in some relationship of complementarity with others. His task, then, was to develop some complementarity, or relatedness. It is a common sign to me that a recovering addict is in danger of returning to drug use when he is in conflict with most of his environment.

In Gestalt therapy, we understand this boundary conflict to be a normative situation. For addicts recovering for some period of time, the choice between their own and others' experience can feel like an emergency. In Gestalt therapy, we are interested in helping our clients experiment with "safe emergencies." A useful metaphor for the skill of attending to the addict in this struggle is that of surfing. As the therapist, I have to feel the current and swell of the client's energy and figure. Pushing him or her to differentiate too early can be experienced as taking something away, and might result in the addict's feeling the necessity to choose between therapist and other parts of their recovery support system, such as twelve step groups or programs. However, if I do not try to anticipate the wave break, I may lose opportunities to help the client explore this crucial process in therapy.

In working with clients at this stage, I have found some particular questions helpful. To support the addict's identification with others, it may be useful to ask, "How is that phrase, meeting, or group helpful to you?" A question that supports interpersonal differentiation would be, "What does that word or slogan mean to you?" Or more pointedly, "How are you different from this person or group?" It is important to place these questions in the context of the addict's recovery.

For many readers, the idea of fostering similarities and not initially emphasizing differentiation may seem counter-therapeutic. But most addicts are quite adept at emphasizing how they are different. If the addict is beginning to view him or herself as similar to others, particularly in terms of drug use, then it may be more helpful to support this identification. For addiction therapists and members of twelve step groups, on the other hand, focusing on differences may seem dangerous or heretical. My experience has been that addicts will differentiate; it is an ongoing and normative growth process. Any approach to working with addiction, and with recovering addicts in particular, needs to attend to these two poles of interaction: identification and differentiation.

Task: Boundary Flexibility and Redefinition

Following the stage of developing some relatedness to others is the development of a more flexible boundary. In Gestalt therapy, we consider flexibility to be healthy, as it offers more choices and thus supports differing needs. A flexible boundary is one that can allow both contact with others and attention to self; it can enable a person to experience both *Thou* and *I* simultaneously. For many addicts, this type of flexibility develops in recovery. If it does not, there is a tendency to move between polar bounding styles, from a rigid, overbounded focus on self as distinct from others and environment to an overly permeable, unbounded merger with others and environment. Typically, addicts tend to live out of this polarity during recovery.

When in crisis or under stress, they tend to flip back and forth between these two poles.

Addicts sometimes engage in conflicts with others, acting out one of these poles and perceiving the other as the opposite pole. Some examples of roles established in this dramatic enactment are the excessive addict versus the controlling spouse; the AA sponsor who carries the abstinent pole versus the one being sponsored who only wants to drink; and the therapist who wants the addict to loosen up versus the recovering addict who is terrified of losing it if he or she relaxes. I believe that the preponderance of examples of this oppositional process is due to the reality that we all carry this polarity within us and therefore can act on it quite easily. In fact, clinicians in addiction treatment work may be prone to engage without awareness in this kind of standoff, because of their own histories and family-of-origin issues.

The problem with all of these examples is that they obscure the addict's awareness of internal polarity: How do I interact with environment and others? How do I bound them out and focus on myself? It may be that addicts are adept at spotting others who fit these poles, or that others gravitate toward the addict's extreme style, or both. From a field theory view, both self and others cocreate the field. What is important in working with addicts is to help them to develop awareness of their way of bounding and to learn to exercise this awareness when they make choices. The addict's task is to develop self-awareness and to develop supports to test out new ways of relating to self, to others, and to the environment. As mentioned earlier, the ways in which we relate to others are grounded in our history. Any work with addicts focusing on boundary issues tends to evoke early life experiences.

Polarity, as used here, refers to the "contact functions" of the boundary in the field, the way addicts organize and relate to environment and others. I am consistently using both words, *environment* and *others*, because the addict's boundary struggle is not just with people but with things (drugs, alcohol, even loud external sensations). The manner in which addicts use drugs is often the same as the way in which they take in opinions, warmth, and anger from others. They either swallow whole and become inundated, or hold out others and their environment as they do with drugs when newly sober. One way to look at long-term recovery is as a movement from I-it to an increasing relationship with others, I-thou. When using drugs and even after, addicts tend to treat people as things, objects to be manipulated.

Addicts often objectify themselves, and report "feeling like a person again" when newly sober. To try to describe the experience of addicts only in the language of interpersonal relationships does not address the depersonalizing experience of the addict. In the following section, I elaborate on this polarity and provide clinical examples of therapeutic interventions.

Addicts are rigid and overbounded when exclusively focused on self as an object to be controlled. This stance can be seen in the individual's holding his or her body in a compacted manner. The belief that goes with this stance is, "I need to do it myself."

John was a client who had been sober for three years. As he entered my office, I noticed his whole body was tense, as if poised to leap into action. His chest barely moved as he talked to me about how difficult his life had become. He said that he thought about drinking but "was determined not to do it no matter what anyone else did or said."

John was in the mode that AA members refer to as *white knuckle* sobriety; that is, he was holding on to himself through sheer determination, becoming more frustrated by the moment. He was building up energy and would likely soon erupt. As we talked, I suggested that he breathe into his chest. He replied that he couldn't or he would fall apart. I appreciated how intensely John was holding himself and decided to identify the polarity of his bounded behavior. I asked him, "So what if you fall apart?" Through a torrent of tears, John told me how he had been let down by others every time he stopped "doing it myself." His rigid, overbounded style served the function of preserving John, because he believed that others would not do so. The downside of this style was that he cut himself off from possible external support. His sensations became like a pressure cooker creating more charge as he redoubled his efforts to "hold it all in."

Eventually, John did try to experiment with breathing into his chest, which he described as a "leap of faith" (in me). From this point in the session, John cried, yelled, and vented his frustration at involvement with others. By having his objections to contacting others supported, John was able to own how he was retroflecting, and to experience the difference in himself when he let go. He also saw that his overbounded style evoked thoughts of using. He recognized that "much more of that, and drinking would have looked good." Later in the session, I asked him to re-create his tightness. As he did this, he moved into a larger piece of work about how he'd learned to hold in his chest whenever he was frightened and left alone as a child.

When addicts are underbounded, they do not discriminate what is self and what belongs to others. The boundary is porous and overly permeable. This is fairly common in addicts during early recovery, or in the stage of introjection-fusing. Betty was a newly sober addict who began to describe this underbounded mode to me in our first session. She began the session by saying, "I know it sounds self-centered, but everything feels like it's about me. Everyone in my home group is angry with me." In fact, everything Betty said was about others, or was something someone else had told her.

It was clear to me that Betty needed to be able to experience herself as distinct from others and not always so central to conflicts around her. To do this, she would first have to experience herself. I asked her if she could feel herself sitting in the chair right now in my office. After wondering aloud if she could, she began scanning her body and noticed that she could not feel her own back, although she knew "it was there somewhere." I suggested that she stand up from the chair and sit down a few times, while paying attention to her back. This was intended to help her break her confluence with the chair, to feel a boundary. After standing and sitting several times, she reported that she could feel more of her spine and that "it hurt." She then changed her statement to "I hurt." Her face flushed and she repeated the statement as if discovering her own experience, "I feel hurt."

I suggested that she take one more step and describe anything she noticed about me or my office that she was sure had nothing to do with her. She observed that I was sniffling and remarked that I must have a cold. I suggested that she stay with her double awareness: "I hurt and you have a cold." She then stated that her hurt was her own, but that my cold was not her fault.

"Are you sure?" I asked.

"Are you kidding?" She laughingly replied. Betty was then able to talk about how hurt she had felt by others in her group. She proceeded to experiment with additional statements about them, which included both an "I" and a "you."

In both of these examples, the result was a movement away from a fixed polarity of bounding toward a middle ground. Our starting point in both cases was the way in which John and Betty experienced themselves in the present. The work that we did was twofold: First, I suggested that they move, breathe, or speak in certain ways, in order to heighten or increase their awareness of what they were already doing. Second, I offered optional stances: statements for them to try on with the intention of helping them consider alternative behaviors. These two approaches are hallmarks of the Gestalt therapy method: focusing on *what is* and experimenting with *what we might do*. My stance with both these clients was curious and experimental, rather than one of forcing my own preference.

The ongoing work for many addicts is to develop these middle ground options, including all the possibilities between the two polar stances of "I have to do it all on my own" and "We are all the same." Finding a middle ground allows individuals to differentiate various feelings and experiences—such as anger, hunger, sadness, grief—from the action of using drugs. In the cases described here, we did this by defining both sides of the boundary through increased sensation. This work involves simultaneously the *individual's cultivation* of his or her own sensation, and an *interpersonal* exchange. For the addict, this is precisely the boundary he or she must work to develop.

Task: Interpersonal Competency

As a result of living in complementary relationships and learning to expand and flex their boundaries, recovering addicts can achieve a sense of interpersonal competency, a process of fluidly interacting with others. What is fluid is the addict's ability to make contact with others yet maintain a sense of self, a skill that supports an increasing variety of choices and behaviors for him or her in recovery.

Many recovering addicts tend to experience their choices as dichotomous, either for "me" or for "you." Interpersonal competency is the capacity to negotiate both our self-needs and our ongoing embeddedness in a field of others. This competence is based on subskills that include the ability to support and ground self, to clearly express one's own experience, to accurately receive others' experience, and to negotiate between self and others. Individual, couples, family, and group therapy can be most useful, sometimes essential, for recovering addicts to develop the above skills, and the therapist's focus in sessions is to help clients learn and practice these behaviors. The Gestalt notion of contact as a full awareness of self and others will be illustrated by the following example of therapy with addicts in this task of recovery.

Melanie, for example, is an addict recovering for ten years, and a member in a ongoing therapy group. Recently, Melanie and another group member, Nancy, had a conflict concerning the direction of the group. Melanie had strong feelings but couldn't seem to express them.

She would try to explain herself, but wind up talking about how Nancy was "wrong." Melanie was unable to repeat what had been said to her, which left Nancy feeling "unheard."

I asked Melanie to take some time attending to her own feelings and thoughts before she spoke. This was novel for her, since she'd always spoken "off the top of her head," but she agreed to try. I also asked Nancy to think about what she most wanted Melanie to hear. When the two of them began to speak again, their pace was much slower, and Melanie was able to express her difference. Nancy stated what she wanted Melanie to hear. They still didn't agree—but they articulated their feelings more clearly and felt satisfied with their interaction.

This result is an example of contact, of the clear awareness of self and other. Melanie had experimented with a skill, checking in fully with self as the basis for communication. Her statements to Nancy were as full of emotion and passion as before, but she no longer felt frustrated. Nancy had the experience of being heard and disagreed with. As a system, they moved from trying to convince each other to hearing each other's experience.

Task: Cooperation

Movement beyond the intrapersonal level continues as addicts become more involved with the world around them. Many recovering addicts become highly involved in service to twelve step programs by sponsoring other addicts. This is often seen as helping other addicts remember their own past, but if we look at the behavior from the perspective of levels of system, the addict is expanding his or her boundary in the field to include concerns beyond the self alone. Frequently, recovering addicts become involved in community activities as diverse as Big Brothers, environmental groups, and political campaigns.

In working with addicts at this stage of recovery, there are a number of options I have used. First, I often suggest that recovering addicts explore their connection to larger systems in group therapy. I make numerous observations of the group as a whole, regarding how the group operates as a system. I encourage individuals to look around the group for support. For example, I might observe to the group, "There is a pattern in this group of individuals of doing their own work while the rest of the group listens," or "Each person in this group helps to cocreate the norms of the group by his or her behavior." These observations are intended to build awareness in the group of how each member cooperates to create the whole. For addicts, this offers the opportunity to consciously influence and be influenced by the whole system. This experience can become paradigmatic for the addict's relationship to larger systems outside of therapy.

This development of awareness of self as part of larger systems is a novel experience for many addicts. There is a tendency among recovering addicts to focus on self, often out of fear and a lack of awareness of others. The movement to being part of something greater than self can be at once both frightening and exciting.

In individual therapy, I have supported the addict's movement through this stage by encouraging the client to focus on his or her relationship to larger systems. I remember working with Ted, who after years of sobriety had begun to think of himself as part of a neighborhood. He wanted to get more in touch with this level of connection. I suggested that he close his eyes and picture his neighborhood. Once he did this, I asked him to picture himself walking around, to look at people and take in his experience. He did this easily, and was soon greeting his neighbors. At one point, he began to tear up. When I asked him what he was experiencing, Ted told me he was remembering his neighborhood as a young boy, when he wouldn't talk to anyone and always kept his head down because he was so ashamed of his drunken father. The experience of holding his head up allowed Ted to see his part in the greater whole of his neighborhood. The following week, Ted told me that he'd actually walked through his current neighborhood, carrying on conversations with others, even stopping to help a neighbor catch his stray dog. This experiment allowed Ted both to explore his interrelatedness with the larger system and to experience his past history of alienation from his environment.

STAGE THREE—LATER RECOVERY: EXPANDING SELF

The third stage of recovery focuses on the experience of moving beyond immediate feelings and reactions to observing self and later observing and experiencing self in relation to all systems. The recovering addict in this stage learns or develops the capacities to observe and reflect upon self, and to transcend immediate feelings (while continuing to feel). This is the stage of recovery where the addict develops deeper meanings of existence.

The therapeutic focus in this stage is often to support the client in developing these deeper or transcendent meanings. It is important for the therapist to discriminate between recovering clients as merely talking about their lives from their actually being in life, yet able to transcend or understand. Themes that are most common in this stage are reexamination of life, changes in career or relationships, and the meaning of illness and death. In this way, these themes parallel those of middle and later adult development in the general population. The difference often has been that the recovering addict may have had a direct experience of these benchmarks in life during active addiction. Second, long-term recovering addicts are often keenly aware of what they have lost due to their use of drugs.

Task: Reflection and Contemplation

As addicts continue to develop more behavioral options, they are able to attend to self in less action-oriented modes. One of these modes is the process of reflecting more fully on the meaning of their experiences. Referring again to the ideal cycle of experience (Figure 1.1), this skill is analogous to the later part of the cycle. This stage is what Wilber calls the *formal reflexive*: the process by which addicts can think about their thinking and the world. It is an introspective mode and crucial to the development of a spiritual practice. In Gestalt therapy, we can describe this stage as awareness of one's own process and the ability to consider self.

For addicts, this stage is often a difficult one, because much of their behavior has been an avoidance of considering self, through desensitization and focus on others. Reflecting is not a process of shutting down sensation but rather the result of "staying with the experience" and not acting on it. Each preceding stage or phase of the recovery has provided the ground for this level of awareness and attention.

Here is an example from my own practice: Stephanie had been sober for ten years. She had been in a series of relationships and jobs that ended with dissatisfaction and pain. Through the therapy process, she decided not to enter into another relationship until she could get a sense of what she was doing. In our work, we explored many different viewpoints to try to describe her experience: codependency, feminism, family reenactment, and others. While she found these somewhat useful, they didn't quite match her experience. Stephanie put it most clearly, stating "I've read these books and they kinda fit but they are words on a page . . . I can't connect."

We collaborated on an experiment where Stephanie would describe certain experiences she'd had, and then make short statements that began with "As I see myself doing that—" She came up with many completions to the sentence: "What I think about myself is . . . I'm lonely . . . I don't trust my own ability to survive . . . I often don't pay attention to how this person or job will fit into my way of living . . . I'm doing what I think I should be doing." This reflection led her to a larger piece of work, defining how she sees herself over time. To do this, Stephanie had to develop the ability to slow herself down to a reflective mode. Thanks to our earlier work, she was now able to reach this mode because she could tolerate sensation and awareness, and so could stay with a difficult issue long enough to forge its meaning to her own needs. Her increased capacity to step back from her immediate experience (feelings, sensations) supported Stephanie in observing her own process.

Task: Transcendence

The last stage is the addict's transpersonal experience, by which I refer to those aspects of the field that go beyond the self and others to connect with all levels of systems. Alcoholics Anonymous describes the relationship between the alcoholic and his or her "higher power" as crucial to the recovery process. There has been some discussion of the spiritual aspect of recovery in traditional psychological literature. Recently, the self-help literature for addicts has focused on spiritual development from a variety of perspectives, stressing meditative practices. There is also controversy about the necessity of religious practices in recovery. Groups such as Rational Recovery criticize AA's reliance on a higher power, believing it deemphasizes the addict's individual responsibility and choice making.

I view spiritual practices as different from religion in that they are inherently personal and not necessarily aligned with particular beliefs or traditions. Spirituality can be seen as another mode of contact, one that is both of the self and beyond the self. Recovering addicts live in a world with others; they are part of systems larger than their own thoughts or schemas. As I think of spirituality for the addict, I believe it to be a continuation of the process of both being a self and going beyond a self. This stage is based on the earlier stages in recovery, in which the addict takes responsibility for his or her behavior by developing different behaviors.

Faye, for example, was sober for ten years before she returned to church. She had been praying and meditating for most of her period of sobriety. But her emphasis in recovery had been on taking action. She was concerned that religion would be a passive experience for her. To her surprise, Faye found that she felt connected to other members in the church and had a sense of mutuality in prayer. She described her experience as praying together rather than praying alone; she experienced her previous spiritual practices as moving her beyond herself to a sense of something more than self, which we might call transpersonal.

For addicts, an integrated spirituality can be a continuing recognition of their limitations and the resulting question of relying on support from others can be part of contact functioning. This stage is a return to the theme of trust, to the developmental conflict of support. For the addict, the ongoing struggle is: Can I trust others to support me? Part of this struggle is realizing that we are, at times, unable to do everything for ourselves; that maturation involves transcending our own thoughts, patterns, and feelings. It is this transcendence beyond the exclusive self that is most healing for the addict. Spiritual practices, such as prayer and meditation, allow addicts to place themselves, *literally,* in the position of trust—lying on the floor, kneeling, sitting in meditation. I believe it is the physical position and practice, as well as the content, that transforms the addict beyond the self.

I am thinking of a client who would not let go of any unfinished situation. For example, if someone said something to him, he would ruminate for days over what that person might have meant. He often felt he had to be doing more to ensure outcomes. He would go over situations from every perspective, exhausting himself. What he came to one day while sitting in my office was the awareness that he couldn't do anything more to control an impending interaction; he had done it all and was still agitated. He said: "I feel like lying down on the floor and giving up." I suggested that he try this and notice his experience. He did so, and I noticed that he held himself up from the floor, appearing not to allow the ground to support him. When I commented on his posture, he began to tear up and his mouth shook. Gradually, he was able to relax into the floor, letting his shoulders drop until he was horizontal. We talked about his experience and he described how different he felt having something other than himself to support him.

This vignette illustrates the theme of trust as willingness to accept support. For addicts who either totally support themselves or demand total support from others, the new behavior is to let go. For this man, the transpersonal experience was to allow the ground, the world, to support him, to risk falling through the floor. It is more than relaxation. This behavior is based on a risk and on the developing belief that beyond himself, something will support him.

Spirituality has been viewed with disdain by some therapists as an avoidance of personal responsibility or as projection. While this may be true at times, it is also a legitimate contact process, and not always an avoidance of contact. It can be the ground for interpersonal support, and a safety net for walking the high wire of life.

In therapy with recovering addicts, we are often faced with clients who talk about their spiritual practices. This later stage of recovery is more than talking about spirituality, more than saying prayers. It is the embodiment of the trust that began in early recovery. In this stage, the recovering addict can release concern for constant self-management. This release is a flowing with the world, a capacity to see the unity between self and the world.

Our task as therapists is to support this development and to provide our clients with behavioral observations. I have taught clients fuller breathing techniques to support their meditation. I have also become familiar with numerous spiritual practices. Our struggle as therapists can be to appreciate the largest level of system and our clients' connection to it.

The stages and tasks described here can give a map to the recovering addict's development through life. Some recovering addicts may never need therapy as a support for their development, at least therapy in the formal clinical practice. But many do come to therapy and are often at a loss to name or understand their struggles or themes. Being aware of these stages and tasks can help us give these clients some context for their experience. The therapeutic interventions described here are based on my understanding of addiction as a self-modulation and of recovery as offering the opportunity for more flexible and potentially expanding boundaries with others.

In the next chapter, I describe case examples of addicts in various stages of recovery and clinical approaches in working with these clients. The tasks of each stage as outlined here are highlighted as clinical issues in working with recovering addicts in therapy.

Recommended Reading

Alcoholics Anonymous World Service. (1976). *Alcoholics Anonymous.* New York: Author.

Bateson, G. (1971). The cybernetics of self: A theory of alcoholism. *Psychiatry, 34,* 1–18.

McConville, M. (1995). *Adolescence: Psychotherapy and the emergent self.* San Francisco: Jossey-Bass.

Perls, F., Hefferline, R., & Goodman, P. (1951). *Gestalt therapy: Excitement and growth in the human personality.* New York: Julian Press.

Trimpey, J. (1989). *The small book.* New York: Delacorte Press.

Wilber, K. (1986). *Transformations of consciousness.* Boston: New Science Library.

CHAPTER FIVE

Five Case Studies
in Recovery

he following case studies follow addicts through the
process of recovery, beyond sobriety. These cases depict the stages and
tasks of recovery as described in Chapter Four, and illustrate recovery
as the moving away from a focus on self into larger spheres of life,
while staying rooted in the fundamental ground of sobriety as a base
for personal development.

Some of these stories are of clients I have worked with as a therapist; others are based on interviews or discussion with addicts in treatment. Each person's path in the recovery process reflects his or her
own personal ground as well as the common process of the stages of
recovery.

DEVELOPING SENSATIONS
INTO AWARENESS

Robert entered a treatment program at twenty-six. His drug history
was extensive, having begun at fourteen when he first smoked marijuana. In the last three years, he'd been injecting amphetamines, and
had progressed to using large amounts of the drug, which caused him

to experience hallucinations and extreme paranoia. Robert was sus-picious of everyone when he entered treatment. He paid careful atten-tion to the nuances and implications of language, and appeared permanently on guard against others.

Robert's treatment experience consisted of addiction education and group therapy, the most common approach for addicts. This group supported Robert to accomplish the first task of recovery, maintain-ing abstinence. He was initially distant in the treatment program but soon began to interact with other patients. For Robert, it was easy to do what he called "talk the talk," that is, to adopt the jargon and style of interaction in whatever system he entered. This chameleon style was one that Robert had begun to perfect as a teenager, and he'd become so adept that his behavior was often outside of his awareness. I was working as a group therapist at the treatment program Robert had entered, and substituted for Robert's therapist one afternoon. As I listened to him talk, I was struck by the seamless ease with which he answered all the questions group members asked.

After one such interaction, I asked Robert what he felt when he spoke to people. He stopped, almost frozen in his chair, and said, "What do you mean?" I told Robert that while I could appreciate what he said, I had no sense of what he felt when he spoke. We went around in circles about this for a while, with Robert asking me to define in detail what I was saying to him. I finally stopped and asked him, "How do you feel talking to me right now?" He took a long time to answer, his eyes widening as he stared at the floor. Finally, he looked up at me with his eyes still wide:

"I don't like it . . . I feel like you don't believe me!"

I told Robert I didn't know what to believe when he spoke. His words made sense, but I had no sense of him when he uttered them. Robert became angry with me and stated that he was doing everything on his treatment plan. He demanded to know what else I specifically wanted him to do—he wanted to stay clean and not go back to his "crazy life."

My interventions were focused on developing Robert's sensations. He still interacted and experienced himself in the abortive cycle of quickly moving into action. Instead of acting by using drugs, the action he now took was to talk without attending to his internal expe-rience. He talked "off the top of his head," his means of adapting the short cycle of addiction into verbal behavior. The task we worked on was to develop his sensations, from which he moved away so quickly, into a fuller awareness of himself.

I listened and let Robert vent all of his anger, perhaps for the first time since he'd started treatment. When he finished, I told Robert that he was right; I did want something from him or I wouldn't have mentioned his behavior. What I wanted was for him to notice how he felt when he spoke. For example, how did he feel now when speaking to me? He looked around the room at the group, his eyes widening and dilated.

Focusing his gaze on me, he said in a low voice, "Scared of being cornered. When somebody corners me, I come out swinging." I told Robert that was how our interaction felt to me. The impact of this exchange on the group was significant. They began to talk about the difference in their experience of Robert when he became angry, and one group member said that for the first time, Robert sounded like one of them.

Robert's style of going along with the treatment plan and speaking in the jargon of treatment is not uncommon. In this situation, it was clearly both his style as an addict—who tended to be on guard—and the norm of the treatment system. By asking a simple question, I challenged this norm of talking jargon without any mention of feelings. Like many recovering addicts in early treatment, Robert would often preface his statements with, "I know what I need to do—" This apparent clarity of self-awareness was a veneer of control through which he ignored his inner life. The disadvantage of this compensation or "as if" style was significant for Robert. First, Robert could not feel or acknowledge his fear and uncertainty. But these feelings can't be avoided forever, and inevitably he would experience feeling unsure without the support he'd need to move through the experience. Moreover, this style of talking "as if" created a distance between Robert and others, as evidenced by the group's assertion that they felt they didn't know him.

Five years later, Robert made an appointment to see me in my private practice. He had remained sober since his treatment experience. He was active in Narcotics Anonymous and had married a woman who was also a member of that program. It wasn't initially clear to me what brought Robert to therapy; I couldn't get a sense of his need. This time I chose to listen and to let Robert talk about himself without interruption. What stood out to me was how relaxed and grounded he looked. He sat comfortably in his chair and used my name when he spoke. Eventually, Robert talked about how he still felt guarded even in his marriage. When I asked what he was guarding, Robert smiled and said he knew I would ask that. He told me that he had always been bisexual. His wife often asked how he was feeling while they made love. When this happened, he was consumed with a fear that she would find him out.

Remembering our interaction in treatment, I said "Do you feel cornered when this happens?"

"Yes," he said, "and I feel like I'm doing some of the same things I did when I was using: lying, pretending, and talking so she won't know me."

He was clearly in middle recovery, having established complementary relationships with others. His present task was how he managed his boundary with his wife, how much he would tell her. He recognized that he was behaving in an old pattern of secrecy, bounding his wife out of his own experience and sexual identity. He was over-bounded with his sexual identity, and this pattern made him feel pressured and dishonest, resulting in feelings of frustration and a keen awareness of how he was behaving. Robert was able to experience this acute awareness because he had developed his sensations, and was no longer numb to himself as he'd been in early recovery.

One thought that occurred to me as I listened to Robert was how much he had changed. He had shown up at the session and—with no spin on his words—simply told me what he was struggling with. Robert had developed an ability to make contact and had clearly chosen to do this with me. I asked him to continue to express whatever he felt, and he did. What became clear was Robert's life history of keeping part of himself hidden from the world. He had begun doing this with his conservative father, who sent him to football practice with the instruction to "be a man." When Robert began to experience sexual feelings for both girls and boys, he knew he could not tell his father. He learned to say what his father wanted to hear and to keep his feelings to himself. As he progressed to using drugs, Robert relied on this ability to remain invisible from the police. When he entered treatment, Robert's style of contact fit perfectly with "following the treatment plan." And now, Robert was aware that he was being the same way with his wife. I asked him what he wanted, and he said he wanted to know how to tell her about himself.

Robert's work in therapy went rather quickly. He had come with a clear need and wanted to explore how to solve it. We worked through this process with Robert using me as a consultant as he spoke to his wife in the empty chair. Almost immediately, Robert saw his father in the chair and he became angry. With passion and through tears, Robert confronted the ghost of his father, who was always with him, and who was clearly the raison d'être for his guardedness. After this session, Robert went home and talked to his wife about his "lie." She told him that she had already suspected this and wasn't surprised. In fact, when she asked him how he was feeling it was at those moments she was wondering whether he was attracted to her or someone else.

Robert had moved to a stage of recovery where he was able to make full interpersonal contact with another without hiding an important part of himself. Certainly, Robert was differentiating his own feelings from his father's homophobia, and from their mutual pattern of "don't ask, don't tell." The ability Robert acquired to talk to his wife depended on his recognition of her differences from his father. Together, the couple created a new pattern of making contact. Although this was a painful conversation for both of them, with many resulting changes in their relationship, Robert experienced a clarity and comfort with his wife and himself. He had taken the leap from hiding and acting "as if" to being himself more fully with others.

Robert had developed enough trust in me that he could now disclose what had been previously unspeakable and intolerable to experience. The work he did after five years was a continuation of the interaction we'd had when he was in rehabilitation. By allowing his sensation to build into awareness, Robert's sexual identity and his relationship with his wife became the next task of recovery and the focus of therapy. What he also learned was that he had organized himself in response to his father's shaming behavior. He had lived in the world as if his father's response to his sexuality was everyone's.

BOUNDARY FLEXIBILITY AND REDEFINITION

Donna was thirty-five when she stopped drinking alcohol in the late 1970s. She described herself as an "old hippie," referring to her use of drugs and to other aspects of her lifestyle. She had used hallucinogenic drugs (LSD, mescaline) on a regular basis while in her twenties, as well as a daily diet of marijuana. After some hundred *trips* or uses of hallucinogens, Donna had what she described as a "bad trip." Clinically, Donna experienced severe and garish hallucinations and had flashbacks from that experience for a year. She stopped using hallucinogens and limited her drug use to tranquilizers and alcohol, which she drank as frequently as she'd previously smoked marijuana. In effect, what Donna did was to self-medicate herself, using the tranquilizing and depressant drugs to diminish the intense anxiety and fear she felt when she tried to sleep.

When Donna stopped using drugs, she entered both AA and NA. Her early involvement in twelve step programs was one of following directions and immersing herself in the experience the same way she had with drugs and alcohol. She became a regular at many meetings and focused her entire life on recovery. Donna would even wear T-shirts with twelve step program slogans to work and social gatherings. The only literature she read was from AA or NA. Donna appeared to have undergone a complete conversion from an actively drunken lifestyle to that of a twelve step monk (a lifestyle described in more detail in Chapter Six).

After about five years of abstinence, Donna took a job working at various times of the day, swinging from evening to day shifts. Initially, she enjoyed the work because it involved helping other addicts. But the changes in her daily structure of work and sleep began to disorient her. She slept progressively fewer hours each evening. Donna felt as if she were leaving her body, an experience she'd often had when using LSD. This sense of detachment scared her, and she felt as if she were doing something wrong. She went to meetings but didn't discuss what she was experiencing. Donna's whole field had changed from a benign place of mutuality to the unreal world she had experienced on her "bad trip."

Eventually, Donna began to hallucinate and was diagnosed as having a psychotic episode. Fortunately, she was treated with an awareness of her history of hallucinogenic abuse. She was given a small dosage of Stellazine, and after a few days of hospitalization, she recovered quickly from her temporary hallucinosis. She was discharged from the hospital and referred to me for individual therapy.

One experience that soon struck Donna was that some other recovering addicts began to consider her as different. She had been hospitalized and was perceived as being on drugs. She felt guilty about using medication, but was so frightened of what had happened to her that she felt she had no other choice. Some people even accused her of being high at meetings, and these exchanges hurt and angered her. The experience led Donna to question much of what she had so adamantly believed and professed to others. Unfortunately, this a common example of how recovering groups and individuals can react to psychiatric medication. Because of their intense focus on the boundary of keeping drugs out, group members tend to see addicts who need medication as threats and often ostracize them.

It was a difficult time for Donna when she began individual therapy with me. Much of the early part of my work with her involved helping Donna to reconsolidate her boundary. She had been so rigid in her relationship with others, yet after she became psychotic, Donna didn't know what to hold on to. She lacked faith in her own ability to stay clean, and wasn't sure who her friends were in the twelve step programs.

As I listened to Donna, I felt moved by her fear. In getting sober, she'd built a kind of wall around herself. By walling her past away, Donna repressed her dissociative process and thus allowed herself to function adequately on a daily basis. For the first time, she'd begun to feel part of a group; the wall she'd created as her own boundary was her compulsive and almost ritualized adherence to the twelve step programs, and she literally didn't let herself feel anything other than gratitude that she was sober. Donna had become abstinent and retroflected too well—she not only didn't drink, she didn't *feel*. Hers was a classic reaction formation of moving away from one extreme by thoroughly embracing the opposite.

When her self-awareness changed as a result of her psychotic episode, Donna was no longer able to maintain her rigid boundary. I wanted to make sure that I supported Donna in gluing herself together rather than in pushing herself toward further differentiation. With Donna, I emphasized any small experiences that fostered consistency, certainty, and continuity: the things she knew about herself rather than the ones she was unclear about, the definite sensations she got from taking a deep breath, the ability to speak of herself as a coherent "I" or "me" rather than as "my parts." We avoided any ways of working that might fragment her more, such as empty chair work.

The other important concern for me was that Donna not create another wall, a rigidly defined identity that might later shatter. I shared these concerns with her and suggested that she might need to develop a more flexible sense of herself. She tried on different metaphors, until she suggested the metaphor of a willow tree that can bend with the wind but not snap. I wondered if she had been a different tree before. Donna nodded and said, "A big, old black oak." This metaphor became the working map of Donna's therapy, and she set it up as a framework within which to articulate her recovery. She used words like "compensation" and "control" when she talked about being the oak tree. Eventually, she was able to discuss the "winds" she faced in her life. She described herself as having "outside" and "inside" winds, and her inside winds were the ones that scared her most. I asked her to describe these and she spoke mostly about her drug experiences, including those where she'd acted impulsively and put herself in danger. Donna had never articulated her feelings of how she'd lived when using drugs. She told me she was afraid she'd get high again if she did speak of those feelings.

My emphasis in working with Donna was to highlight, in very concrete ways, what she knew about herself. To do so, we had to return to developing sensation, exploring ways of knowing that ranged from Donna's touching her face as she talked to me to expressing what she knew about her past. I wanted to help her find her own experience in small, distinct units of work. Donna had postponed this process of self-definition in recovery, in part because she was afraid of what she would find. In terms of recovery from addiction, Donna's experience was not uncommon. To differentiate herself from others, she needed to congeal within herself, to become more solid. Donna's increasing consolidation of self showed over time through her increased physical relaxation in unfamiliar situations, through her newly developed ability to express personal experience and emotions in her own language rather than in program jargon, and through her comfort in letting others know what she was feeling. She had learned that she could weather any winds by being flexible and still maintaining the stance of her recovery.

LEARNING TO BE RATHER THAN DO

Mark got sober at forty-five after thirty years of drinking. He had progressed from drinking at parties on weekends to daily drinking and wet lunches. He was introduced to Alcoholics Anonymous by an old family friend who'd been sober for twenty years. Mark had gotten to the point where he didn't want to stop drinking but couldn't tolerate the consequences, which included liver pain, a lost marriage, and a habit of waking up in strange places with strange people and not knowing how he'd gotten there. When he attended his first AA meeting, Mark had the sense, for the first time, that he was not different from others. He also felt that this feeling of identification might be an answer to his dilemma of drinking; there were many people at the meeting who'd once drunk the way he did, and who were now abstinent.

As a young boy, Mark had grown up with the specter of a domineering and magnetic alcoholic father. Although he hated how he'd felt when his father was drunk, Mark deeply admired the man's professional power and ability to influence others. Like many children of alcoholics, Mark set out to differentiate from his father, yet emulated him in his double-breasted suits, powerful business position, and double-bourbon lunches. When he stopped drinking, Mark was faced with his similarity to the father that he both feared and admired.

An early issue for Mark in recovery was to think of himself as a professional who didn't drink. He initially felt insecure, as if "something was missing" when he would go to lunch with clients and not drink. His experience was as if an arm or leg were missing. Mark began to talk about this experience with the older members of AA who were in business. He needed to see himself through a different lens; through these relationships, Mark began to develop this new lens, that is, to learn a different way of living and working.

In looking at this process, I think of Mark as meeting two needs through these interactions with older businessmen in AA. He clearly was gaining a new experience of how to live in the world without alcohol. At the same time, Mark was being fathered in a dynamic he'd never had with his own father. These relationships created a strong bond between Mark and AA. He saw himself as a part of a group of men who were living their lives in a productive fashion. For Mark, sobriety and the social support of AA were the answers that had been missing from his life.

From the time he stopped drinking, Mark did not have an urge to drink again, which is uncommon for alcoholics who drink for the length of time Mark did. He attributed this to his identification as an alcoholic, and to the immediate changes he experienced when he began living the AA program. It was as if he had returned to the early values he'd learned as a boy in church: honesty, fairness, and taking responsibility for his behavior.

Mark joined a therapy group because he was curious about "what you all did in there," and because his AA sponsor suggested he needed something more than meetings to help him with his relationships. His entry behavior in the group was to try to help others by giving advice and telling them about his experience. I was working as a coleader in this group and felt initially irritated by Mark's interruption of other members' work to give advice. The group also felt annoyed with Mark and told him this directly. He was stunned by this feedback and responded by dropping his head and tightening his jaw. In that moment, my irritation faded into a kind of gentleness for Mark. I asked him, "What are you doing, Mark?"

He looked up and his face had turned red: "I'm doing what I always do in groups. I share my own experience and try to help other people." Mark was behaving in a way that was the norm for an AA meeting and was trying to connect with others in the best way that he knew, but he clearly had no idea how to make contact with others aside from being advisory and helpful. Two of the group members started to ask Mark questions about what he was experiencing, and he remained bewildered. Finally, he looked at me and said, "What do I do?" What seemed most important was to take advantage of an opportunity for Mark to interact with others differently. I responded that he might ask people in the group what they wanted from him. He seemed pleased with this advice and proceeded to ask everyone the same question: "What do you want from me?"—like a boy trying out a new bike or fishing rod.

This interaction became quite effective. Diane, a group veteran of many sessions, said to Mark, "I want you to tell me what's going on with you when you tell me about your past . . . I want to know about your feelings, not just the events." This had a great impact on Mark; his face again reddened and he began to tear up. He talked about his desire to "do things right and not screw up!" We closed his experiment of hearing from the group by asking Mark what he'd learned. His answer was that the group wanted different things from him than the ones he was trying to give them. This was a revelation for Mark: to hear how far off base his projections of others were. He spoke of feeling ashamed of not doing things right. I asked Mark what was shameful about not always doing things right. This led him back to his fear of making mistakes in front of his father, who'd screamed at him when he did. My interventions with Mark concentrated on his sense of himself, in particular the extreme value he placed on accomplishing tasks according to some internalized standard. Mark was clearly in middle recovery, focused on how he experienced himself in relation to others. My intention was to encourage Mark to be reflective, to consider how he thought of himself and what he believed others expected of him.

Mark stayed in this group for a year and became a valued and active member. His emphasis still remained centered on what he could do, on the action part of life. This had been true when he drank and worked long hours, and was now the way in which he approached therapy. About three years after he'd left the group, Mark called me for individual therapy. He was now about eight years sober, and his need was to slow down. He had been diagnosed as having high blood pressure and was frequently tired. Mark had evolved from the stage of focusing exclusively on action and on what he could do for others, to a readiness to pay more attention to himself, a development typical for a man in his forties. It is also an evolution for Mark, as a recovering alcoholic, to reexamine the emphasis of his life from action to a more reflective ground. It is the beginning of the spiritual-transpersonal stage, and is also characteristic of Mark that it took high blood pressure for him to consider changing his focus and style of living.

Because of his personal readiness to change, it took very little intervention to get Mark to slow down. Our work together was minimalist. I taught Mark how to meditate by breathing slowly and deeply into his abdomen and to extend his breath. Mark called this process "learning how to *be* rather than *do.*" We would spend entire sessions breathing together while holding our hands on our bellies, so as to feel ourselves breathing deeply. He continued this process for a few months, and returns for checkup appointments every now and then.

Mark is an example of an addict who got sober by following a specified method. He learned to do what his sponsor told him. He frequently would ask me for advice or suggestions. Sometimes I would offer behaviors for him to try on, always following up by asking him what *he'd* learned or experienced. At other times, rather than suggesting possible action, I paid exclusive attention to what Mark was experiencing. This initially confused him, as he was so used to following directions. But he developed an ability to stay with his experience and eventually began sessions by stating, "Now, I'm not asking you what you think I should do—I just want to talk and see what comes up for me."

Mark has moved from introjecting from others to taking responsibility by staying with his own experience and developing his own figures. His is also a transition from seeking father figures to fathering his own experience and ideas. The focus of his life is no longer not drinking, although he remains active in AA. Mark's focus is now on himself as member of the community. He is clearly in the community stage of recovery, experiencing himself as part of a society of people. In our last session, I told Mark how impressed I was that he had made the commitment to become a Big Brother to a fatherless teenager. He thanked me and said, "You know, when he asks me what I think he should do, I ask him what his thoughts are before I answer."

IN MY OWN EYES

Patti grew up in a small town where the main industry was the steel mill. Everyone she knew worked in the mill and attended the Catholic Church. She remembers longing for the affluence she saw on television.

In contrast, her family seemed to be continuously struggling to make ends meet. There was never money for anything more than the basics of food and functional clothing. Patti would watch television and read magazines about Hollywood, and dream about how different her life would be.

Patti began smoking cigarettes with her best friend when she was thirteen. She was caught by the nuns at her Catholic school and sentenced to detention for a week. This experience only served to embolden Patti more; she began to see herself as an outlaw, an image that satisfied her desire to be different from her small town family.

She was fourteen when, smoking cigarettes after school, her friend offered her a beer. Patti drank the entire beer in two minutes. The feeling that soon enveloped her took away all her awkwardness and made her laugh. This was the trip out of the small town she'd been craving; she felt sophisticated and beautiful all at once. Throughout high school, Patti drank on weekends and sometimes after school. She was not immediately obsessed with alcohol, but enjoyed the feeling that it gave her. Patti was attractive and worked after school in the mall to make money to buy sophisticated clothing. She always looked perfect to others, wearing beautiful clothes and behaving as she had seen actresses on television behave. When she drank, her experience was that she could "pull it off" with greater ease. She acquired a group of friends who drank on weekends with her, and they would talk about moving to the big city and getting great jobs, driving fancy cars, and living in elegant condos. In many ways, Patti behaved and thought as a normal adolescent. The major differences were that she loved to get drunk and had developed a persona based almost exclusively on her appearance and on an acquired manner of interacting with others.

Patti followed her dream and moved to the city after high school, first attending college and then working as a paralegal in a law firm. She began using marijuana at parties and soon was using alcohol or marijuana on a daily basis. For her, these drugs served as a social lubricant, allowing her to feel sophisticated and not small town. Patti became involved in a series of relationships with men, mostly professional, who supplied her with more of the veneer of a successful, upscale woman. She never managed to feel this way when not high, so she continued to use more frequently. These relationships often ended when Patti realized she didn't like the man very much. She felt comfortable but always somehow different, unknown by the partners she continued to make for herself. It was as if she longed for something more than the goal that she had achieved. She wanted to be herself but felt terrified to risk it. The volume of her drinking increased, and she began to use cocaine in addition to her daily marijuana.

During this period of her life, Patti moved three times to a succession of beautiful homes. In the last home, she and her new husband spent huge sums of money redecorating. The night they moved in, Patti's husband found her drunk on the kitchen floor, crying about feeling empty. He was surprised that night, and progressively less surprised for the three years their marriage lasted. He'd fallen in love with the person Patti appeared to be, and she'd let him see nothing beyond the practiced veneer she had created. By the time they divorced, Patti was drinking daily and in large amounts. When intoxicated, she could no longer hold back her feelings, but began to express her true sadness, anger, and loneliness. She would often make trips to her home town to feel "comfortable," but always with a bottle or a stash of marijuana at hand.

Patti hit bottom when she could no longer drink as much as was necessary to diminish withdrawal. She had gotten to the point where she would become anxious if she went an hour without some alcohol. She managed to get a prescription for tranquilizers to help her maintain her equilibrium, but was arrested for drunken driving one evening when she was both drinking and using the pills. Following her arrest, Patti was placed in a hospital where she went into alcohol withdrawal. This was an enormous surprise to her, even though she had been a daily and heavy drinker for over ten years. She began attending AA meetings in the hospital at the encouragement of her physician, and identified herself as an alcoholic. For Patti, recovery began as a physiological necessity; she could no longer drink the quantity necessary to avoid withdrawal symptoms. She'd remained unaware of her own problem, perhaps because being an alcoholic didn't fit with the image she had created for herself years ago as a teenager.

Patti soon became an active member of AA and remained abstinent for eighteen months. In AA, Patti gravitated toward men and they to her. She continued her pattern of relationships with men as cover for her internal experience of shame and inadequacy. She went to the beach with a new male friend, and when he offered her a marijuana cigarette, she smoked it quickly. Patti stayed in this relationship for over a year, sometimes still attending AA meetings but continuing to smoke marijuana on a regular basis. Her behavior made her feel dishonest, but she continued trying to keep her feet in both worlds. Aside from going to a few meetings, Patti had little human contact with anyone except her lover and a few other drug-using companions.

Eventually, this relationship ended and Patti returned to AA. This time she connected with women members in the program, and these relationships had an enormous impact on her sense of self. She felt initially frightened and angry with the no-nonsense approach of the women; she'd grown used to a less direct way of communicating with men. But after a period of time, Patti began to have some of the first in-depth conversations about herself that she'd had ever had. In the past, she'd been content to allow men to project onto her and her attractive appearance, with no mutual interest in her talking about how she felt. This time she was in interpersonal systems where the focus was on contact with self. Patti began to talk about her true experience of herself rather than simply projecting the acquired sophistication; she discussed her sense of inadequacy and feelings of stupidity. While her sense of herself didn't match what others perceived, what was important was that Patti managed to express these feelings for the first time in her life. At the urging of her AA sponsor, Patti had no sexual relationships with men for over a year. She saw this period as one of important growth, when she focused on herself rather than how others viewed her.

After nine years of recovery, Patti entered therapy again at the urging of her sponsor. She had been feeling depressed and at thirty-nine was feeling old. The relationship was significant for her since she chose me, a male therapist, a choice that offered her a chance to develop new boundaries with men. The task for Patti was to define herself in relationship to another, whom she perceived as more competent than she. I was supportive of her exploration but very clear that I was interested in her internal experience. During this work, Patti began to reexperience the anger and shame she'd felt as a child, attending church in old clothes and having to steal to buy things for herself. She was again struggling financially and felt frightened that she had to make it on her own. I asked what was wrong with that, and Patti responded that she couldn't do it. I asked how she'd made it to this point, and this led to a number of sessions where she explored her own self-support. Often she would get stuck and ask me "What should I do . . . what do you think?" Usually, I smiled and said something to her like, "What makes you think my choices are any better than yours?" Patti became enraged at me for not helping her, which led to her anger at her father for not taking care of her when she was a child, for drinking away much of his small paycheck. Much of her work in therapy focused on her anger with her father, with men, and often with me. My stance of staying with her when she was angry created a clear boundary at which to experience herself as engaged with another. Such an intervention was an important experience for her; after ten years of recovery, she could allow herself to feel her anger.

Three years after this work, I received a card from Patti at her new business, a catering company she and a female friend had started. She was excited about her new business; she felt she had become successful, and joked with me that she sometimes went to work without makeup or even without washing her hair. She has remained continuously abstinent for over eight years.

Patti is an example of a woman who needed to stop using drugs to change her life. The second change that she made was to examine her interpersonal relationships, and to determine whether they supported her own development. The mentoring relationship with her woman AA sponsor helped her develop a new vision of how to interact. For her, to stop drinking and using drugs was not as difficult as to stay abstinent. To do this, she needed to tolerate the feelings she had long ago desensitized through drugs and through the admiration of others, particularly men. She developed clear boundaries—first with drugs and then with others—a task that helped her develop a sense of her own identity as a woman, rather than to see herself through men's eyes.

Patti made use of therapy when she'd reached an impasse in her recovery and life, which was the frightening recognition that she was getting older and that she looked different. With the help of therapy, she was able to do the work of the reflective stage of recovery: attending to herself with some perspective beyond her immediate sensations.

IN IT FOR THE LONG RUN

Agnes got sober at forty-five, after twenty-five years of heavy drinking. She had managed to maintain some standing in her community and a marriage that produced two children. Her immediate family and friends were relieved when she stopped drinking. Her behavior when drunk had been difficult for those around her. Agnes's husband continued to drink, however, which created a conflict in their lifestyle. They had been drinking partners, buddies who would take off for long periods of time on "road trips." She entered a detoxification unit that allowed her to safely withdraw from alcohol, and that introduced her to Alcoholics Anonymous. After leaving the detoxification unit, Agnes began attending AA meetings, which also interfered with her time with her husband. Because she no longer drank, Agnes's husband was forced to continue his sprees on his own. Agnes began to involve herself in the lives of her children: attending teacher conferences, returning to church and Sunday School, and even volunteering in Girl and Boy Scouts. She later described these experiences as "boring me to tears, but I knew I needed to give something back to my children."

As Agnes continued to do more on her own without her husband, she felt more competent and asked him less for advice. While for her this was an empowering experience, it represented another differentiation in her marriage. Her husband became increasingly critical and angry at her when he drank. Agnes's sobriety and newfound independence were too much for him to tolerate. After a number of fights and arguments, her husband filed for divorce, which she did not contest. Their marriage had been a closed system, functioning best when both participants were intoxicated and away from everyday social structures and responsibilities.

From the perspective of addiction, Agnes's husband could not tolerate her abstinence; it made his continued drinking more obvious. Not only had he lost his drinking partner, but he was constantly exposed to alcoholics who were not drinking. Agnes, once she'd stopped drinking, had little in common with her husband and preferred to use her energy to develop common ground with others. Agnes never remarried; she raised her children as a single parent. Her husband died of alcohol-related liver damage.

As Agnes began to make more contact with herself and others, the system of her marriage became less important to her, and she felt more confident in her ability to live on her own. She would sometimes feel nervous or frightened, and even thought about how a drink would make her feel better. But she learned to "think the drink through"— that is, to think the action of drinking through to its familiar conclusion and ask: "What will happen to me if I have a drink?" She accomplished the task of retroflection almost immediately in her recovery.

Agnes joined a therapy group for recovering addicts during her first year of recovery. The focus of this group was on developing mutual support with other recovering addicts and to learn social interaction without alcohol and drugs. The main intervention by the group therapist was to focus Agnes on her sensations, to encourage her to stay with her feelings of anger, fear, and sadness, feelings Agnes had anesthetized for years. She was able to make this change through the support of group members struggling with the same task. The major theme that emerged for Agnes was her fear of people. When meeting others, she often experienced a combination of excitement and anxiety over anticipated outcomes. Like many recovering addicts, Agnes imagined and worried over how another might respond to a particular choice of behavior. Working in the group allowed her to feel these feelings and to experience the *actual outcome* of an interaction. During her drinking, she'd simply medicated herself so as to not feel the dreaded outcome, or else she'd avoided the interaction. At the cusp of each interaction she felt a twinge of shame, and another result of her work in the group was for Agnes to identify and decrease this sense of shame.

Agnes continued to remain sober and to attend AA meetings, and yet felt unfulfilled. She had finished college as a young woman mostly as a social function. But now she felt a desire to do something with her life. After five years of sobriety, at the age of fifty, Agnes entered an MBA program. While remaining involved in AA and parenting her children, she finished the program on schedule. She saw this as an important achievement in her life: "I was more than somebody's wife or daughter . . . I was a businesswoman professional." Clearly, Agnes had not developed her own professional identity as she had not developed a sense of herself as a mother until she stopped drinking.

Later development of professional identity is not uncommon for women. One influence that has been cited by Sheila Blume is gender-based roles and social identity. For Agnes, this was clearly the case. She reported that "I never thought of myself as working . . . I thought I would get married and that would be that." What facilitated this struggle was her return to therapy, individual therapy with a woman therapist. The therapist consistently asked Agnes about her career interests, which raised Agnes's awareness that she did, in fact, have professional interests.

Drinking had clearly influenced Agnes's identity, as had the collusive drinking relationship with her husband. When Agnes stopped drinking and her husband continued, she was forced to differentiate. Her own needs and desires became more figural, more important to her. Alcohol and other drugs deaden awareness, as do certain kinds of relationships. Agnes's development as a woman with a career (in the home and outside) emerged when she ended both these desensitizing patterns. As she later described this experience: "When I got sober, I woke up to a lot of things . . . my life . . . my children . . . and my marriage. And I didn't like a lot of what I woke up to."

As Agnes stayed sober and remained active in AA, she became a mentor to younger women alcoholics. This process occurred gradually, starting in her fifth year of recovery. She was seen by them as an example of a mature recovering woman. This became a large part of her life, talking with and advising these women in restoring their lives after drinking. In many cases, Agnes was able to support and to guide them in going on to college or graduate school and in developing careers. She was thus able to provide for others what had been given to her: guidance and vision. This is one of the long-term stages of development for addicts, as it is for adults in later development. In contrast to her drinking life, which was not focused on others, in recovery, Agnes became increasingly involved in others' lives, an involvement that represents the middle stage of recovery; as Agnes became more involved with the world around her, she increasingly saw herself as an integral part of a community of women.

Agnes had been raised in a formal religious family, but as she described, she'd only gone through the motions. After joining AA, she began to pray and meditate, initially to ward off her desire to drink. Over time, she began to feel connected to her prayer and meditation and reformulated her spiritual beliefs in a different manner. She had always viewed God as a critical male figure; however, by the time she was ten years sober, her view of God had changed to a benign spiritual presence who guided her.

The first time I met Agnes she was about fifteen years sober. I was struck with her wry sense of humor and her willingness to speak frankly, her directness and the way in which she was willing to learn from others. We worked together in an agency and though I was twenty-five years younger than she, she would often ask me what I thought. I remember asking her about her openness and she laughed. After a long pause she said, "Well, how else am I going to learn anything new?"

When Agnes was twenty years sober, two events occurred that continued to shape her spiritual view. Her only daughter was killed in a car accident at the age of thirty, leaving behind her two children and husband. Agnes had been an involved grandmother for five years, but the loss of her daughter was the catalyst for spending more time with her grandchildren. Her experience was one of overwhelming grief that initially caused her to question much of her life. Agnes returned to therapy to deal with this loss. According to her, "I worked on a lot more than my loss. My therapist kept asking me what meaning I made of this experience." Her therapist focused Agnes on the recovery task of reflection and transcendence. Agnes's loss was framed in the context of a mature recovery, based on her capacity to support herself and to seek and make use of support from others. If this loss had occurred during Agnes's early recovery, when she hadn't developed the functions of retroflection and boundary flexibility, the therapeutic focus might have been on how Agnes could survive this loss without drinking. When the tragedy occurred, she had thoughts of drinking, but did not. They were transient thoughts; Agnes remained involved with AA and supported her family through this crisis. In a sense, she was able to transcend her own feelings to see the large system around her: her grandchildren, her friends, and her family.

As with all lives, Agnes's had a final chapter, the last gestalt. She was twenty-five years sober when she learned she had a kidney disease. She took this with the grace and courage with which she'd survived divorce, her daughter's death, and other losses. Agnes made the best of the time she had left, remaining involved with other alcoholics and with her family. At one point in her suffering, she said, "I've had enough." It was not long after this that Agnes died, after twenty-seven years of recovery. In a sense, her life was that which she was impelled to develop, cultivate, and expand after she stopped drinking. She had grown up in recovery, moved out of her own self-focus and embraced the world. My last conversation with Agnes was on the phone in her hospital room. She was still clear and direct with me. We spoke about this book and about her grandchild. When I asked her how she was doing, she answered me with characteristic clarity: "Michael . . . I am ready for this to be over . . . I have lived a good life." I've thought about her final statement and amidst my tears and sense of loss, I am struck by Agnes's integrity and honesty.

I've presented Agnes's story last because she is an example of an addict who moved through the stages of recovery. Agnes consistently attended to her own boundary with alcohol, yet did not remain fixed at that point. She moved beyond herself to reconnect with her own family and with other systems in her life. In a sense, she created a new family or system with other AA women.

Redefining her identity as a woman was an important part of Agnes's recovery. As she developed more collaborative relationships, Agnes changed her vision of herself. In recovery, Agnes began to reflect upon herself as different from the role in which she was raised, and in terms of what possibilities she might pursue. Similarly, her spiritual development was not based on the introjects of what others told her, but on her own integration of her past and on disciplined practice.

—⁓—

These individuals came from a variety of backgrounds. Some of them had advanced education and ongoing relationships at the time of their recovery. Their families ranged from highly supportive of their recovery, disinterested, to unsupportive. Their developmental themes in recovery ranged from self-esteem to sexual identity to professional identity to spiritual struggles.

An early point for all of them was identification of their inability to control alcohol or drugs after some period of attempting to manage their intake. This was the beginning of their recovery; identifying addiction as avoidance of sensation and recovery as restoration of sensation and the capacity to move beyond sensation. Donna and Mark moved through the early stages of identifying as addicts and building a firmer boundary with alcohol or drugs. For them, the challenge in recovery was to relax their boundaries so as to take in more from others, to trust more, to engage more, and to allow others to support them. To accomplish these tasks, they had to acknowledge their fears and doubts and to let go of having a programmed answer for everything. In a sense, they had to go beyond ritual and repetition to experience the varieties of their own and others' experience.

Agnes felt no confidence in her own capacity to work in a profession. This theme became an important task in her recovery, both a form of interpersonal competence and cooperation. Mark struggled with accepting the experience of slowing down and tolerating a pace in life that he previously would have considered boring. Both Robert and Patti carried a sense of shame in their recovery. This sense of shame and an accompanying lack of trust influenced their contact style and the way they organized their interpersonal field. It was only after naming and experiencing this sense of shame that they were able to engage in the larger interpersonal field. The development of contact skills in therapy, such as slowing down and grounding, focusing on the environment and developing clearer boundaries, helped these recovering addicts change the way they organized their world. In therapy, these clients created a different field in which to explore these themes.

These case examples are of addicts of some considerable length of recovery. They illustrate the stages and tasks of recovery. In the next chapter, I will describe some specific issues of addicts who recover for long periods of time.

Recommended Reading

Blume, S. (1985). Women and alcohol. In *Alcoholism and substance abuse: Strategies for clinical intervention*. New York: Free Press.

CHAPTER SIX

Long-Term Recovery

The Expanding Horizon

~~~

Recovery as I have defined it is a developmental rather than a chronological process. One addict can be abstinent for twenty years yet still remain in the first stage of recovery; another can progress to the third stage in less than ten years. This chapter focuses on long-term recovery and its relationship to the previously outlined stages of recovery, particularly second- and third-stage recovery. As defined in Chapter Four, third-stage recovery is the continued expansion of the addict's contact skills and capacities to include larger systems of interaction.

Third-stage recovery involves the tasks of reflection and contemplation and of transcendence. A key aspect of the task of reflection and contemplation is the recovering addict's identity as a field-related phenomenon. But as throughout the rest of recovery, long-term addicts may move through prior tasks at a deeper level as part of their growth. For example, addicts in long-term recovery, upon reflection about their roles in relationships, may return to work on interpersonal competency in those relationships. Such an integration is not uncommon; many long-term recovering addicts engage in meditation and review of their life. Therapy can also be the catalyst for such a return as well as a forum to explore these issues. In long-term recovery, addicts are often forced to explore aspects of their personal and professional identity.

Descriptions of addicts and their integration of aspects of identity tend to share some common continua or polarities of existential choice inherent in long-term and third-stage recovery. The addict's process of choosing to live in recovery through these continua is often the task and background of the therapy.

The ultimate choice of long-term recovery, as in any life, is whether addicts continue to expand themselves and their interpersonal field rather than attempting to maintain self and the interpersonal field as static. When working with addicts, why refer to their experiences after fifteen, twenty, and twenty-five years of abstinence as recovery? Why not merely call it life or personal growth? I believe that the growth experiences and lives of addicts have a particular meaning and process. Each addict's life experience after abstinence is unique, embedded in that individual's movement away from intoxication and toward expansion of the interpersonal field.

The more recent emphasis on addicts as recovering is rooted in two aspects of the addict's post-abstinence experience. Many treatment specialists and AA or NA members began using "recovering" to emphasize the belief that an addict can never drink or use again—that is that there is no cure other than one based upon abstinence. Fingarette and other theorists citing research suggest that this may not always be the case, that some alcoholics can drink in moderation. This data may be related to the overdiagnosis of addiction in cases of substance abuse rather than dependence. My clinical experience has been that addicts who return to use are often able to do so in moderation for a period of time. Eventually, however, the true addict will return to the addiction cycle. The importance of maintaining recovery from addiction as an ongoing process seems to rely on the awareness of one's own limitation.

My own clinical experience has been to work with dozens of people who forget and have returned to using. I have attended funerals of overdosed addicts and know a number of alcoholics who lost their livers due to relapsed drinking. The theoretical speculation about addicts returning to using must be balanced by these experiences. I have also worked with some so-called alcoholics who drink periodically for years with no appreciable problem. My own stance is to never encourage drinking or using again but to deal with this experience when and if the person returns to treatment. For a true addict, the process and progression of abuse and consequences will renew, and we can hope that the person will seek help.

The larger question here is why professionals need to support drinking or using. Are drinking or recreational drug use necessary social skills? While there are clearly false-positive addicts, we as a culture feel some discomfort with limitations. Addiction is a limitation, yet over time it does not have to restrict or limit social, educational, or interpersonal functioning. The only limitation for addicts is their inability to manage drugs and alcohol.

RECOVERY AS AN ONGOING PROCESS

In terms of the Gestalt notion of figure development, we speak of some awareness becoming figural, contacted, and then closed. Upon closure, this awareness becomes part of the ground or existing background for the next figure. What is background helps shape our experiences in the future. For addicts, the potential for returning to drug use seems to remain as part of the background. This is usually true as they move out in the world and gain some sober time. The addicts' background awareness of the experience of addiction casts their lives in a new shade. They may have had the experience of nearly dying or have seen others die from addiction and therefore appreciate the fragility of life. Having frequently lied, they may now be attuned to truth; or having gone to extraordinary lengths to use drugs, they may appreciate the range of human behavior. The addict's past, held as piece of the background of everyday living, is a rich ground of experience and a kind of innate wisdom.

An important quality of recovery is the way in which individual addicts carry their past in their awareness. If addicts don't remember how they used the drug, felt about themselves, or any of the varied consequences of their drug use, they may drink or use again, convinced that they are different now. Clearly, forgetting is different from holding an awareness in one's background. In contrast, if addiction is always in the foreground of an addict's awareness, then other aspects of life recede. Such an addict develops less awareness of others. Addiction becomes an obsessive process, with the same concern arising daily. This kind of pattern in recovery creates an impoverished field, one in which recovering addicts may feel bored or limited in their choices. It can also lead to feelings of despair and cynicism where the addict can only view people and experiences through the lens of addiction. I remember an old heroin addict, Sid, who perceived everyone's behavior as a form of conning or "getting over." Even after a year of recovery he couldn't believe that anyone would tell the truth or would offer anything without expecting something in return.

Another reason for the use of *recovering* is to emphasize the whole of the addict's life rather than to focus exclusively on the boundary issue of drugs. As I have described and as the case examples illustrate, the drug is merely a method of self-modulation gone amuck. To use AA's language, the drink (drug) is merely a symptom of the problem. Terence Gorski and Merlene Miller describe the primary goal of recovery as "learning how to live a meaningful and comfortable life without alcohol or drug use." The stories in this book as well as the literature of recovery support the idea that recovery is as much about personal development and healing as it is about abstinence. This then is a larger set of tasks of recovery: to develop the addict's capacities for contact with self and the world. It is in developing capacities for contact and expanding the field that the recovering addict develops.

IDENTITY DEVELOPMENT

As addicts stay sober longer, individuals differ in the sequence and emergence of certain identity themes. Many addicts may have already resolved or developed some of these aspects of their identity prior to the use of alcohol or drugs. Many of these are life themes, experienced differently among individuals over the years, which evolve as addicts recover a fuller existence. As one recovering addict interviewed after twenty-two years of recovery put it, "Who I am, what is my purpose . . . that's the big question." The identity themes described here are typical of some addicts in long-term recovery, and exemplify the tasks of reflection and contemplation and of transcendence.

Identity as a Process of Experience and Reflection

Identity can be thought of as the way we think about and experience ourselves over time. It is part of our ground that we only come to know at the boundary of our contact with others. We define our identities in terms of behaviors or activities as well as by our association with certain groups. This identity may change depending upon what group we are in at any given moment. I believe there are some pervasive beliefs we carry about who we are, our identity. We may announce this identity when we speak about ourselves "I'm the kind of person who—" or "I'm a—" In introducing ourselves, what is the first thing that we say to others? Do we say "I am a recovering alcoholic"? "I'm a psychologist"? "I have two children"? "I'm a Leo"? Whatever we say or believe about ourselves is what we identify as "I." From this perspective, I would continue by defining self-esteem as how we value our belief of who we are.

Addicts who are proud of their recovery and the changes they've made in their lives may feel pleased when they think of "I" as a recovering addict. In contrast, other addicts may feel shame and social discomfort when thinking of themselves as addicts. They may also carry introjects from others about what it means to be an addict, which might range from moral judgments and contempt at one extreme to romanticizing and admiration at the other. Part of the long-term work for addicts is to integrate *their* experience of themselves. These feelings or values are certainly embedded in the social context in which the addict lives.

Frequently, therapists have a different attitude toward this identity than does the addict. Often this difference is a projection or attribution of what the therapist would feel if he or she identified as an *addict*. Or often, when the therapist is also a recovering addict, the client may have to differentiate from the therapist's experience.

I remember a colleague who liked to describe himself in a cheery manner as a "grateful recovering alcoholic." Perhaps he actually felt that way, but often his clients didn't. A client who had been in recovery for ten years once responded to this therapist that sometimes he felt grateful, sometimes sad, resentful, or blessed. This client was able to integrate his own experience rather than feel he had to comply with the therapist.

For addicts, the sense of self has been intertwined with being intoxicated, or looking forward to or recovering from the experience. This process is so pervasive that addicts are sometimes unaware of who they are if not a drunk. The more often addicts use, the more they will think of themselves in this way. It becomes part of their ground, part of who "I am." Self is experienced in a desensitized and withdrawn manner. Other aspects of life and self (relationships, education, profession, spiritual life) will increasingly be crowded out by the use of drugs. Who I am becomes smaller and smaller. Often in early recovery, addicts ask, "What will I do if I'm not drinking or using?"

As addicts stay sober for longer periods of time, thoughts of and desires for the drug become less dominant in their lives. There is room for them to experience self in other ways. This is the restoration of life and contact functioning that occurs in recovery. In short, we are what we do, who we are with, and where we have been. If we change what we do and come to accept and finish with where we have been, then our sense of who we are changes. If addicts change their behavior, then their identities will change. This change comes from the addicts' completing cycles and assimilating new experiences. The ground of self reconfigures like a kaleidoscope shifting in the viewer's hands; the interacting forms create a new whole. So it is with recovering addicts who shift their understanding of self and contact with others, creating new visions in recovery.

Recovering Monk

Some long-term addicts don't seem to develop self-identities other than "I am an alcoholic." The most glaring example of this was a man I knew who would identify himself as "I'm alcoholism and my name is Bob." Every time I heard him describe himself in this way, I was curious about what else he knew of himself. I was also struck by how Bob described himself as an example of a syndrome rather than as a person who was also alcoholic.

But Bob is not unusual, even though his self-description is extreme. Many recovering addicts identify themselves exclusively in terms of their addiction. These addicts sometimes don't talk to nonrecovering people at all. They live their lives in twelve step—a choice different from attending meetings or therapy to support living life *outside* of meetings. When using, the addict associated with other using addicts or those who would tolerate the drug use. Now in recovery, long beyond the point of identifying and developing a plan of staying sober, some recovering addicts, like Bob, associate only with other recovering addicts as though they lived in an isolated monastery devoted to addiction and abstinence. Significant changes in recovery are put off or never experienced by this monastic lifestyle and narrow self-identity. The monastic addict continues to organize his or her world in a mirror opposite of active addiction: all relationships and meanings are significant in relationship to drugs, in this case, to the abstinence from drugs.

In my practice, these people often come to therapy with relationship difficulties rooted in their inattention and lack of involvement with others. I have found myself concentrating on helping such clients and their partners or families attend to the neglected aspects of their lives: interpersonal relationships, expanding interests, and ways of interacting. I often notice the parts of the kaleidoscope that are missing from the picture.

For example, Fred and Jane came to therapy as a couple because they felt bored and experienced little excitement in their lives, not an uncommon complaint. When I asked them to talk about what they did, all their descriptions were of separate activities. She was a recovering addict who worked and attended meetings, and he had developed a separate life. They had little common ground. In a sense, their sober life mirrored their life when she was using, with the exception of the drug; they were each making their own lives. Jane was frightened of "going outside of the program"; Fred had no desire to attend meetings. To feel some shared excitement, they needed to develop common interests outside the twelve step program. They were able to explore her fears and develop interests that did not exclude her involvement in AA meetings, but that added to this important part of her life.

This is a common scenario. Many recovering addicts stay fixed on maintaining a boundary that supports abstinence and self, often to the exclusion of their families. Clearly, the husband in this example also gained from their bifurcated relationship; he could pursue his own interests without negotiating with his partner. All processes involving groups of people are both maintained and functional in some way to everyone in the system. In cooperation with her husband's detachment, the recovering partner continued to identify herself with twelve step programs and not with her relationship.

Interpersonal Identity

From a Gestalt perspective, our sense of self is developed within the field of our relationships with others and the environment. We don't exist in isolation but as part of a field that is the self-other boundary. As relationships change and the addict's needs change, so do the field and the addict's identity. Many addicts report in long-term recovery that they change their views of interpersonal relationships. After some period of internal work and change, they are more likely to approach these relationships differently than through the fear-control polarity so characteristic of addicts. That early phase of addicts' relationships can be best described by a statement a client of mine made: "I don't have relationships . . . I take prisoners." The conflict between trust and allowing others to behave independently often remains to some degree. Frequently, in order to continue to tolerate the uncertainty in any interpersonal experience, addicts may need the support of psychotherapy (individual or couple). This work focuses on the second-stage task of interpersonal competency and the third-stage recovery task of reflection.

The struggle is often for the addict to allow the *inclusion* of another into the field as an equal *cocreating* partner. For much of their addiction and even recovery, addicts have been preoccupied almost exclusively with self and self-boundary, and thus tend to dominate their interactions and be complemented by a partner who allows this dominance. They may have also been in a system (twelve step group) that involves a high degree of confluence and shared experience. *Who I am* is different from *who I am with you,* and even more different from the larger question of *who we are.* This is the very essence or movement of recovery, beyond the intrapersonal to the interpersonal. As addicts remain abstinent for long periods of time, their roles within family or primary relationships change. The boundaries between and including family members may expand or flex. For any such change to occur within the system, other members of the family have to adjust their own boundaries and roles.

As an example, recovering parents may move into more assertive roles and children who acted as adults may struggle with or be relieved at abdicating these roles—or both. Over time, the recovering partner in a relationship may succeed in a career or develop a strong sense of competency, rather than depending on the partner's competency or identity. These transitions in the recovering addict's identity are also changes in interpersonal identity and the interpersonal field. In long-term recovery, these adjustments are common and sometimes lead to changes in the definition of the relationship, even to separation, divorce, or total redefinition of roles.

In the couples work I've done with recovering addicts, or in couples systems I've experienced through individual one-on-one work with recovering addicts, this struggle has been apparent. If the addict is newly sober, or even after a few years of recovery, the couples work may be influenced by unfinished individual work of the addict's partner. I have frequently suggested individual work in conjunction with the couples work to develop the internal supports for contact or to identify the old business that tends to clutter the field of these systems.

The question of who he or she is in a couple, or as a parent or family member, has some history or ground prior to the addict's use of drugs. Many addicts grew up as children of addicts or in family systems that overstimulated them and failed to provide adequate environmental support, creating what Robert Ackerman calls "emotional disengagement." Frequently, the work that addicts are drawn to do is to separate their own interpersonal identity from that of their family or their role in that family. Family-of-origin work is crucial for addicts to get a clearer sense of how they behave and what their options might be. As a Gestalt therapist, I am interested in supporting this work with recovering clients and want to hold the whole picture of the addict's experience. It is easy and fashionable for adult children of addicts to express their rage at the obvious abuse and neglect that occurs within these kinds of families. But I always want to balance this "no" of anger and separation with the other side, which is the addict-child's desire to be loved by the addict-parent, and maybe even the child's loyalty and attachment to the parent. I can think of numerous examples of clients who feel strongly ambivalent toward their parents. When expressing anger at their parents in the empty chair, I want to honor the complexity of the other feelings, which may include warmth, sadness, pity, loyalty—equally valid feelings and part of the actual impasse of the adult child. Confronting the ghosts of the past only with anger leaves out the need or longing that was not met. After clients express what they didn't like to their parent, *fully*, I might ask them to pay attention to any other feelings they experience, or specifically, to what they did like. The importance of this recognition for a recovering addict is that it supports the complexity of the relationship and makes a more accurate model for the complexity of future relationships.

Another aspect of this work is that it can help clarify who the addict identifies with as a role model. We learn by watching our parents and family interact. I remember a middle-aged alcoholic who'd reached an impasse in his marriage. We explored this in individual therapy while he continued in marital therapy. Eventually, he was able to recall his father's phrase—"Don't just quit anything!"—and how his father never stood up to his dominant mother. The realization that he saw himself as behaving like his father allowed him to explore in couples work how he was *in relation* to his wife.

Professional Identity

This is often an important aspect of development for addicts as their years in recovery continue. Because of the impact of their drinking and using, addicts are often underemployed and undereducated when they enter recovery. The early period of recovery can be a period of working in jobs that provide no challenge to the recovering addict but provide security in the form of a wage and a daily structure. Some addicts report feeling like they are "giving something back to the world" via their employment.

As addicts continue to recover, they frequently experience a need to develop some kind of profession or career. The story of Agnes in Chapter Five is an example of this kind of later-life development, more common in female addicts than male, as it is among females in the general population. But it is also a theme for male addicts whose professional identity may be delayed by the process of addiction.

Often it takes addicts as long as five years to develop some kind of profession or to enter college or training of some kind. Returning to school can be a stress in recovery; it takes addicts out of their normal routine, and may also require that they spend long periods of time in isolation while studying. The addict's balance between self-focus and environmental contact undergoes a reformation.

Frequently, addicts maintain some kind of ongoing profession or career throughout their drinking. Such continuity may provide their recovery with a sense of security. But they may also feel concerned that they won't be capable of doing the same job equally well, sober or clean of drugs. Their identity as professionals or workers may need to develop by their repeated experiencing of their competency. Some highly educated and trained recovering addicts may appear to feel immediately competent upon returning to work; yet these same addicts in therapy often discuss feeling doubts.

After some period of recovery, many addicts who have begun with careers seek to change their professions, a syndrome that can be compared to midlife development in the general population. It is as if their identity changes through sobriety. Edward is an excellent example of this process. He had worked in banking and Wall Street during his drinking and his first ten years of recovery, at which point he decided that this activity—which he called "hustling"—was no longer consistent with "Who I am in the rest of my life." He sold his business and moved to Key West, where he now paints and works with other recovering addicts. Edward's vision of his life changed as he grew in recovery. His sense of himself as a professional changed along with his vision, and he moved to reconcile this difference between his vision and how he was actually living.

This example is more dramatic than most experiences, but it illustrates how professional identity for addicts over time changes with the addict's whole life view. We might also describe this movement as toward the spiritual or humanistic plane. It may also be the result of working at a profession for some period of time. Some women addicts with whom I've worked developed their professional identities later in life, and consequently attach a different meaning to their careers than might someone who'd maintained a profession throughout adult life.

As Kate, a recovering addict of fifteen years, said: "It never occurred to me that I could be a professional person in the world." Kate is embedded at the community stage of recovery where she is experiencing her competency as a professional in the world and is thus developing that which is emergent and untapped in her identity.

Sexual Self

Sexual identity is often another important aspect of a recovering addict's development. Addicts often feel less inhibited under the effects of alcohol or drugs, and can thus be more sexually active when intoxicated. Some addicts continue the same pattern of sexual behavior after sobriety as when using; others struggle during recovery with a homosexual identity, which intoxication disinhibited them enough to act upon. As one recovering addict described, "Alcohol cut the tension of my conflict about being homosexual."

Arthur drank heavily throughout his addiction and could then have sexual contact with men. If he didn't drink, he felt "overwhelmed with guilt and a fear of being caught and losing my job." After he stopped drinking, Arthur could no longer attain the immediate release from his inhibitory feelings. For years during recovery he would cruise parks and public places to find sexual partners. Because he couldn't bear for people to see him as gay, he never developed a relationship. After fifteen years of recovery, Arthur entered therapy saying that he felt "phony" and frustrated by his lack of interpersonal relationships. Although Arthur was in his forties, our work together was similar to therapy with a younger gay man who was just coming out. I attended to Arthur's fears of what others would think and say about him, which led to his recognition that he made these same judgments about his own sexuality. He'd begun drinking at thirteen, about the time his sexual urges were beginning to emerge. Arthur had used alcohol to modulate his sensitivity to others and their judgments of him but also to desensitize himself to his own conflict and judgments about his sexuality. By drinking to modulate these conflicts, Arthur delayed integrating his sexual identity. This delayed process then became the theme of his therapy.

In therapy, Arthur explored his feelings about homosexuality, society, and the way he thought about himself. This was painful work, as his self-judgments were extremely harsh. In Gestalt language, we would describe Arthur as having a big *top dog*, a critical aspect of self that criticizes and dominates. The final part of Arthur's work was to identify and own his top dog. I asked Arthur to say what he usually thought about himself as a gay man. When he voiced these thoughts, he became aware that his own verbalization matched the way in which his father had spoken to him. He always felt as if his father were watching him when he had sex with a man, and he top-dogged himself to keep himself in line just as his father had done to him when he was a boy.

Addicts often continue to seek desensitization and to use frequent sexual interventions in the same way that others use a drug. Tom was a client who became sexually active after five years in AA. He literally preyed on new women in the program, engaging in brief sexual interactions. He often didn't want to know his partner's name and described that he would feel numb immediately after orgasm. Tom was re-creating the same desensitized pattern of his narcotic use. He experienced quick, intense sensations, acted habitually to get what he wanted, used it, and withdrew until the next urge.

He experienced himself and his partners as objects rather than as individuals. His identity was in his sexual attractiveness, the first part of this cycle. By continuing in these short, abortive cycles, he never experienced the uniqueness of his partner, or his own possible feelings of fear, longing, or interest in his partner. This shift became the focus of his work in therapy, what he would experience if he felt himself and his partners more fully. He thought of himself as an object, a tool, just as he had during his active addiction. His body was separate from himself, an "it," something he used to reach a desired outcome. Sex for Tom was an attempt to lose awareness, and he needed to perform it repeatedly in order to stay unaware. In therapy, Tom and I explored his sense of himself as an "it."

One day, after a few sessions, I asked him how he became a tool. Tom answered that he didn't know, adding that he would think about it. He canceled the next session. Two weeks later, Tom began the session by telling me he had been dreaming about being a tool, a wrench that all kinds of people were using and holding in their hands.

I asked Tom to picture himself in the dream. When he did this, he became very agitated, breathing quickly and moving around in his chair. Abruptly he opened his eyes and said: "I see my uncle and he's making me touch him. He calls his genitals 'my tool.' I can feel myself just go numb . . . I'm not aware of what I'm doing . . . just do it."

I asked Tom how old he thought he was when this happened and he answered, "About twelve . . . right about the time I started drinking."

By becoming more aware of himself, Tom had reexperienced an incident when he was sexually abused. Tom's style of sexual contact and his identity were rooted in that event. He had reversed roles with his uncle, becoming the tool with women, while staying numb in his adult life as he had coped with the abuse.

This theme of sexual identity often becomes more figural when addicts have been recovering for a number of years. My experience with clients is that the presentation of this theme after some time in recovery relates to the need for development of sober ground, a foundation in the focus on not using. Frequently, clients discuss this with their AA or NA sponsor or attend Gay and Lesbian AA meetings as a support for their experience. However, questions of identity or long-term identification as gay or lesbian seem to develop after five years or more. Some twelve step meetings have a distinctly heterosexual group norm, and recovering addicts struggling with sexual identity may feel different or misunderstood. As one recovering addict put it, looking back after fifteen years to that early period, "I wanted to go to a group where I could talk about *anything* without censoring myself, so I started to go to Gay and Lesbian meetings." Clients have indicated that they attended these meetings for a period of time to support themselves in being able to identify as a "gay or lesbian alcoholic," but many did not continue with these groups for long periods. Other clients clearly attend these meetings as a part of their continuing program of recovery.

Another aspect of this struggle is that gay and lesbian social interactions may often occur in bars and nightclubs. Many addicts—

particularly during early recovery—avoid social settings where alcohol or drug use is present, in an effort to diminish temptation and to avoid scenarios that might evoke the pattern of using. This tension between the addicts' need for abstinence and their social needs was described by a client as "I felt like I had to decide, am I alcoholic or am I gay?" These aspects of identity are crucial; if experienced as dichotomous, they can place the recovering gay or lesbian client in a situation of choosing what is more true about them.

TRANSCENDENCE: SPIRITUAL IDENTITY

Addicts often have had a mixed relationship with religion and spiritual practices. Many experience God as a punitive figure, and many are agnostic. Some of the clients I have worked with describe their experience of God or a "higher power" as being like archetypes of their own parent figures. It is as if they have introjected their parents and perceive spirituality through that lens. In sessions with addicts as they grow older in life as well as in recovery, this theme seems to reemerge as it did in early recovery. But in later recovery, the sense of the spiritual is more grounded in a hunger for connection to a level beyond the self, and a need to make meaning of the changing field.

The Fertile Void

In Gestalt therapy, we see the ending of each cycle and the beginning of another as a fertile void, a period of less defined awareness, and a creative moment. As addicts continue to develop in recovery, their capacity for contact supports them in finishing experiences and moving with more awareness into this fertile void. Two themes in therapy tend to emerge as addicts allow themselves to experience this fertile void: toleration for not knowing and acceptance of the inevitability of endings, particularly death. Accepting the inevitability of death as the constant that defines our existence has long been considered an existential truth.

As addicts stay sober in recovery for longer periods of time, they encounter more experiences of others dying or becoming ill. In a sense, to be an addict in a community of addicts is to have death as a background of the stage of life. Addicts die all the time, usually at younger ages than the rest of society when the death is related to addiction (overdose, auto accident, and so on). However, for addicts, dying from addiction is often seen as a result of "not working the program," a way of thinking that supplies a meaning and explanation of death that may diminish anxiety. But death from so-called normal causes, or at an early age, challenges the meaning of recovery as resurrection from a living death.

If we believe in ourselves as the ultimate reality, then to not exist is incomprehensible. To accept death is to return to the experience of horizontality; death is lying down and accepting the process that is around us. It is the ultimate surrender to beyond the self.

DEATH AND GOD

Barbara had been sober over ten years. During that time, she had been involved regularly in AA, and had been in therapy for periods of transition. She entered therapy this most recent time to work with the depression her family doctor had diagnosed. She had recently lost two friends to AIDS and expressed her despair and confusion about that loss.

After we had met for a few sessions, Barbara began to ask me questions about my spiritual beliefs. This was a moment in therapy when I had to choose whether to disclose my own experiences and beliefs. I had been asked many questions, which were often statements framed as questions, and had responded in a number of ways. But Barbara's questions to me were not mere projections, they were genuine questions of her existence. She wanted to know, if she and I were not God, then who was? And where do we go when we die? And if we are really only here (in the flesh) for a short time, then what's the point? She was not panicked or frightened, but wondering about her relationship to life.

I looked away from Barbara and thought. How could I answer these questions? Should I respond from my own experience? I asked Barbara what was making her ask these questions, and she told me that when she meditates, she goes into a "void," a place she remembers from as early as her childhood. She added that when her friend Jim died, he went to the void, and that she imagines she will go there when she dies. I told Barbara that this was as good an explanation as I had, and asked her if she could go to the void now. She smiled and said "Any time," and closed her eyes.

"I'm swimming around in a kind of liquid space and I can feel and hear everyone but it's like underwater. Jim is here too and my grandmother . . . I feel safer as I stay here. I can even float to the top of the room and see you and me talking. It feels like I'm getting past my own body and my fears."

I was moved to tears as Barbara described her experience, remembering my father's funeral and how I had felt as I transcended the entire service. Barbara told me that this meditative experience was what helped her get through her daily living. I told her that I had no answers for her and that I felt she'd answered her own questions. I admitted that I had my own questions and some of my own answers, but that they might not be for her.

She agreed and said, "You know, it isn't really important to me who God is, just as long as I can stay connected to everyone in some way, even without my body."

Barbara needed to reexperience her void to feel more connected to others. But this connection was a transcendent one, beyond her body in a plane of energy. In the ensuing weeks, she became less depressed and was able to weep for Jim's death yet feel she had some contact with him. I encouraged her to continue her practice of meditation. Barbara managed to transcend Jim's death and her own sense of loss through her spiritual practice and her growth past the exclusive focus of "how this affects me." She was clearly going beyond herself, and this journey both afforded her comfort and provoked questions. My stance with Barbara was to clearly support her experience, neither dismissing her meditation as wish-fulfillment fantasy nor joining with her by offering my spiritual beliefs.

I'm also reminded of Andrew, who after seventeen years of recovery developed heart disease and said in therapy, "Is this what I got clean for?" It was as if, after all his struggle to stay sober, getting clean could somehow protect him from mortality. His acceptance of the work of recovery was based on some kind of barter or *condition*. He had believed that if he stayed sober, "bad things wouldn't happen to me." Clearly, death has nothing to do with being in recovery, and addicts don't get to choose the form of their death any more than anyone else. Allowing ourselves to experience our mortality is the experience of transcendence.

Giving More Than Taking

In a similar vein to Barbara's experience are the comments by numerous recovering addicts and clients about transcending their own needs. One client, sober after fifteen years, described her looking forward in recovery to "giving more than I take . . . every day I ask myself have I taken more than I've given." This is another example of going beyond one's own needs or fears. For addicts whose main focus has consistently been on *self*, satisfying self, managing emotions and experience, and keeping a clear boundary with drugs and alcohol (and perhaps others), to give to others without the expectation of something in return is often the result of years of growth.

This comment is an expression of someone who in her life has taken from others, disrupted the balance of the social field by one-sided behavior. To give as part of this social field is to be part of *giving and taking*, rather than merely taking as many addicts do, or giving in order to receive rewards. This latter is often called codependency and is clearly the other side of the same coin as taking. Lore Perls defines a present or gift as "not a sacrifice, but something that is given easily and without expectations on the side of the giver." My experience with many long-term recovery addicts is that this is how they experience their involvement in AA or NA. They often use the term *service* to describe giving to others. When I asked a recovering client why he continued to sponsor so many people, his answer was that he did it for himself. He didn't mean that he was seeking to gain something directly, although some recovering addicts do have this intention. He described the experience of being more comfortable with his world and himself, feeling a kind of "harmony." This is similar to Lore Perls's description of the "present restoring the integrity of the giver as well as the receiver."

These acts of giving are closely connected to spirituality because they are transcendent acts, acts of getting beyond the momentary fears and concerns of self. They do restore balance to the field and support relationships. But perhaps most important, such genuine presents are possible because of the development of a true ground of self. The old AA saying, "You can't give away what you don't have," describes giving and transcending self as based on the ground of developing self.

CHALLENGES: POLARITIES OF LONG-TERM RECOVERY

A recovering alcoholic of twenty-five years once described recovery as being a process where "the ante is always raised." He was referring to new levels of change as necessary for an addict to maintain growth and recovery. The opposite of this is for the addict to become complacent and in a recovery that remains stunted. For example, some addicts who justify unacceptable behavior by saying to self or others, "Well, the important thing is I'm not drinking or using." Many of the examples I have used in this book are descriptions of addicts struggling with the next level of ante. Recovering clients who do not struggle with the ante or who are unwilling to share this struggle rarely come to therapy. Often, long-term recovering addicts perceive therapy as a failure of or disloyalty to a twelve step program.

From a Gestalt perspective, I see maintaining growth as an acceptance and active involvement in the ever-changing field of the self-other boundary. Each new formulation of our experience brings us to a heightened and sometimes painful sense of self and the field. If the recovering addict tries to maintain the field (or recovery) as a static form, a fixed gestalt, his or her energy diminishes. What was once bright and vibrant becomes flat and even frustrating. This is the experience of long-term recovering addicts who don't change or adjust themselves to the changing ante. Often, this frustration can lead to thoughts and actions of drinking or using again. Accepting and experiencing these changes are the challenges of long-term recovery. These challenges differ on an individual basis, and may range from making amends for past behaviors to developing a spiritual practice, but represent similar general polarities or choices for recovering addicts.

As Joseph Zinker and Rennie Fantz describe, human experience can be seen as choices along polar continua. Long-term recovering addicts frequently come to therapy struggling to integrate polarities of behavior, feeling, and thinking. The edge or challenge for these recovering addicts as clients is to be able to move to both ends of the polarity and develop the capacity to learn middle ground options between them.

A polarity that I have been discussing throughout this book as fundamental in recovery involves the way the addict attends to self and others. The process of recovering is the integration of the capacities to attend to self or others and all the middle ground of attending to both. The goal of working with this polarity is to develop the client's capacity for the whole range. At any given moment, it may be useful to be aware of self or to be aware of one's relatedness with others, or even to hold both as part of the field. As Paul Goodman stated, it is important for clients to leave therapy with more rather than less than they entered with. My intention in working with clients is to add options, not to take away their present preferences.

Let's take a look at some common polarities I experienced in working with long-term recovering addicts in therapy.

Expansion————Conservation

There is a tension between two aspects of growth. In each of us, at any given moment, there are forces for sameness or conservation and forces for change. As addicts stay sober for longer periods of time, they frequently have less need for sameness, yet become accustomed to the repetition and comfort of continuing patterns. Individuals who are oriented in this way often preach to others in a dogmatic fashion in twelve step programs. It is as if they are trying to conserve what has been a life-sustaining process and to make it structure their lives.

Miriam is an example of someone who reinforces "how things used to be in the program." She entered a therapy group at the suggestion of "someone I trust." In this group, she wanted to know what the rules were and would often tell younger group members how they should proceed with their lives. When the group questioned Miriam about her *own* reason for joining the group, she initially attributed it to her friend who happened to be her AA sponsor. But this was a sophisticated group, and they pushed Miriam to say *her* reason. She finally confided that she was having trouble with how AA was changing, with all the young people and drug addicts entering the program. She wanted to keep things as she had known them for all these years. But at the same time she knew she couldn't do it; things and people change. She'd become embroiled in a series of conflicts about traditions that meant more than the written guidelines of the AA program but were Miriam's personal structure for the environment. This was Miriam's challenge: to accept the changing field of which she was a part while maintaining a sense of comfort and familiarity.

I admired Miriam; she was a tough woman who'd survived and made many changes in her life over twenty-five years of recovery. The group and I helped Miriam develop an experiment in which she would tell group members what they should do to change. The intention of this derives from Arnold Beisser's theory of paradoxical change; that change occurs by intentionally doing what we already do *but with awareness.* She entered this experiment with her usual relish and was soon standing up and pointing her finger at people, telling them about how they should change.

The group was initially angry but began to laugh at each of Miriam's pronouncements. She went so far with this experiment that she herself began to laugh. I asked her what it was like to give these directions to others and she said, "I'm exhausted . . . it takes a lot of work and they just won't listen." I asked her what would happen if she didn't do it. Miriam became silent for the first time in the group. After what seemed like five minutes she said: "Things will get out of control and I won't get any help." To which I added, "Unless *you* structure it!"

Miriam nodded her head and looked around the group, perhaps seeing it for the first time. She had become aware that her insistence on sameness was for her own sake and required her to exert enormous effort and to constantly scan her environment. Miriam's work in therapy was indicative of the task of reflection; she was able to step out of her immediate experience and to reflect upon her own process and belief system.

Miriam's experience is a common one for long-term recovering addicts in twelve step programs. They are sometimes like controlling parents or grouchy grandparents, railing at the changing conditions of the program. Miriam is an example of someone suffering from what I would call the "twelve step blues" where an individual becomes so invested in maintaining the status of a system that their own process, often an inhibited one, becomes background. Their energy and self-awareness is projected outward to the environment, a process that may be in response to anxiety, fear of aging, unfinished business, or a general lack of success in their relationships, jobs, or families.

Optimism————Bitterness

Bitterness is almost always accompanied by a past-oriented perspective: something has left a bitter taste in our mouths. But for the addict to be bitter in the present is one of the symptoms of relapse; it often leads to drinking or drug use even after years of recovery. I've seen this in addicts who can't accept the choices they've made in the past or present, and who sometimes feel as if they've been passed by in AA or NA.

For addicts, optimism is the belief that possibilities lie ahead and are doable; that they can manage their world. Bitterness is the experience of feeling unfinished and of perceiving the world cynically, as an unfriendly environment.

Tim, who was in recovery for over twenty years when I met him, exemplifies this polarity. He attended a workshop I presented and complained about everything from the chairs to the coffee to the ignorance of the other participants. I was both annoyed and amazed at Tim's audacity. In the latter part of the workshop, I needed a volunteer to demonstrate a concept for the participants. Tim volunteered. He seemed ready to re-create his bitter, complaining role from earlier in the day. I was faced with that conflict that many of us who present workshops are often faced with: the difficult participant.

I agreed to sit with Tim in front of the group. He began the same way, saying everything that he didn't like. I initially felt frustrated with Tim and then began to laugh. He wanted to know what was so "damn funny." I said that I was amazed at how well he could collect such a litany of gripes, I could never do it. I was afraid that I might feel encouraged about something and couldn't stay bitter.

Tim stopped and his face darkened. Finally, he said: "I haven't felt encouraged for years, I'm wiser than that." This led to a discussion of Tim's process of wising up since some major disappointments and pain in his life: the death of his daughter and loss of his health.

Tim had not put these disappointments behind him. He could not look forward with any optimism or hope. He was carrying his past losses around with him like a suit of wet clothes. He is like many long-term recovering addicts, who for various reasons are frozen in their life, bitter about the past. What was helpful in my short work with Tim was for me to respond to his style of contact rather than try to make him feel good or go over the details of his complaints.

Narrow Focus———Widened Lens

This is the polarity described throughout the book: the continuum between experiencing the entire context or system and focusing on a specific within that system, such as on not using or on personal feelings. Both poles are essential for recovery and growth. It is crucial to be able to isolate an issue pertaining only to self such as "What I need to do to stay sober"; it is also important to eventually get beyond self to stay sober and recover. The first of these is what I'm calling a narrow focus while the second is the widened lens, organizing the field beyond self-boundary management.

Caroline stopped drinking at the time of her third son's fifth birthday. She was in the final stages of alcoholism and her recovery was an enormous benefit to her family. She threw herself into the recovery program and spent most of her evenings at AA meetings. Her husband and oldest son maintained the family. When her son went to college, he entered into counseling and began to talk about his childhood before and after his mother's drinking. He felt deserted by his mother *in her recovery*. He confronted her about this, and Caroline's initial reaction was to respond that recovery was what she needed to do for herself. He persisted in telling her about the impact on him. She became tearful as he brought up soccer practices she had missed and his feeling that her friends in AA were more important to her than he was.

Caroline was angry with him for some time. Even after thirteen years, she felt as if she were having to choose between *her recovery* and *her family*. It was only when she became a grandmother that Caroline was able to widen the lens of her awareness to relationships outside of herself and her recovery.

Retrospective————Looking Forward

Examples of addicts who are purely retrospective abound in twelve step programs. The irony is that by talking about their active addiction and focusing exclusively on that process, they may be creating vicarious enjoyment. At least, these addicts may focus exclusively on the past or their drug use because they don't know other ways to socialize. Talking about the past becomes an easy social lubricant, as alcohol or drugs did in the past.

For the addict, there is a tension between a forward perspective, facing the future as a horizon of possibilities, and a retrospective, looking at who and where they've been (that is, active addiction). It is essential for addicts to keep themselves from forgetting what they've done if they are to keep themselves from drinking or using again. This kind of looking back is also an important way for any of us to make meaning of our lives. Life in the present is based, or more accurately *grounded*, in our histories. For long-term recovering addicts, keeping some perspective of their past gives a richer meaning to their growth and development. But the extreme of this is the addict who can only talk about using, who frames everything through the lens of an addicted lifestyle. Long-term recovery is really a balance between the two extremes, as with all the polarities.

Brian provides an example of someone who struggled between these two poles. He was recovering for twenty years and had restored his life from a very severe addiction. Brian entered therapy at his wife's suggestion, telling me, "She says I can't plan for the future. We're getting older and I suppose this is important." In fact, most of what Brian talked about was what he or his life had been like before. I asked Brian what his objection was to planning, and he responded that he thought planning was "projecting," and that he lived "one day at a time."

I was struck by how useful it had been for Brian to keep such a clear perspective of his past. It helped him to not drink and to understand his life in context. But Brian was polarized; he experienced himself as having no future. He thought of himself as twenty-five years old (the age he was when he stopped drinking) rather than as a fifty-year-old husband, father, and soon-to-be grandfather. Brian was not expecting grandchildren; he was, in fact, not expecting anything. When I thought of this and looked at his soft eyes and down-turned mouth, I had a deep sense of sadness.

I asked Brian what he looked forward to in his life. At first, he answered me with explanations of living in today. I persisted and he began to tear up. Finally Brian said, "Well, I have my health and my wife and kids and maybe grandchildren." He said that he knew if he got excited about the future, everything would turn out poorly. That was what he had learned in his recovery: not to get too excited or something bad would happen. We worked with this underlying belief for a number of sessions by looking at where he had learned this as an absolute. It was helpful for him to describe the times when thinking this way was useful to him, such as when he was in early recovery and devastated by disappointment, often wanting to use. The functionality of his belief was clear. What he became aware of in therapy was the limitation of dealing with all his experience from that point of view. A few weeks later, Brian came to a session with an announcement. He told me he had gone to his pregnant daughter and asked her if he could paint the baby's room "ahead of time." I asked Brian what this meant to him and he said, "I couldn't keep acting like we weren't going to have a grandchild . . . so I wanted to prepare for him or her."

Brian had moved to a middle ground between not having a future and projecting. He accomplished this by experimenting with looking forward in his life. This experiment in reflection helped Brian access feelings that he would not let emerge as long as he doggedly looked backward and maintained each day as a soldier guards his post. He still retains his awareness of where he has been. His life has not been lessened, only enriched by broadening his perspective to include all 360 degrees of the past, present, and potential future.

I also recall Henry, a man who lived out of the pole of looking forward. Henry was very involved in recovery, yet had an extraordinarily healthy look at age sixty-five. He was sober over thirty years when I met him. He had taken up sailing in his retirement and would often stop by the treatment center where I worked. His eyes had the look of a man who was watching the horizon, feeling the wind and looking forward for the next shift or change. When he died, I thought about him sitting in his little sailboat, his white hair blowing back and keen eyes checking the horizon. He was literally moving forward in the world while knowing where he had been. Now and then I imagined he would check his wake, that he would talk about his drinking past, but he was pointed away from that into open water. This image of

Henry captures long-term recovery as a journey of making contact with whatever comes *next* while remaining aware of what has happened.

—⁓—

The themes and examples in this chapter offer a vision of long-term recovery as a continued development beyond the self. Some of the examples illustrate recovering clients who, although abstinent for long periods of time, are stuck in some aspect of their own development. In the next chapter, I describe how these kinds of sticking points in recovery can lead addicts to seek the familiar pattern of sensation and action, and potentially to relapse into drug use.

Recommended Reading

Ackerman, R. (Ed.). (1986). *Growing in the shadow: Children of alcoholics.* Pompano Beach, FL: Health Communications.

Alcoholics Anonymous World Service. (1976). *Alcoholics Anonymous.* New York: Author.

Fantz, R. (1975). Polarities: Differentiation and integration. In D. Stephenson (Ed.), *Gestalt therapy primer.* Springfield, IL: Thomas.

Fingarette, H. (1988). *Heavy drinking: The myth of alcoholism as a disease.* Berkeley: University of California Press.

Goodman, P. (1991). *Nature heals.* Highland, NY: Gestalt Journal Press.

Gorski, T., & Miller, M. (1986). *Staying sober: A guide for relapse prevention.* Independence, MO: Herald House.

Perls, L. (1992). *Living at the boundary.* Highland, NY: Gestalt Journal Press.

Zinker, J. (1977). *Creative process in Gestalt therapy.* New York: Brunner/Mazel.

CHAPTER SEVEN

Relapse

I have described recovery as the progressive restoration of contact functioning and the widening of the interpersonal field through fuller sensation, developed awareness, and nonhabitual actions. Relapse, from this perspective, is the progressive and often gradual diminishing of contact. The medical model describes relapse as the appearance of disease symptoms after a period of remission. This is an inadequate focus for the purpose of therapy with addicts. It is a projection of an internal process onto some abstract thing that causes the addict to behave in certain ways.

What we call *relapse* begins with changes in the way a recovering addict behaves, feels, and thinks. The addict alters his or her way of making contact with the environment and self. The relapsing addict's contact style begins to look more like the addiction cycle, only without the drug. Gorski and Miller developed warning signs and a stage process for the return to addiction. These warning signs range from difficulty in thinking to memory problems, irritability, depression, erratic interpersonal behaviors, and withdrawal.

The Gestalt model frames these by illustrating the shrinking aspects of contact, both with self and others. Relapse is a reversion from a fuller cycle or process of contact to the addict's former narrow cycle and focus limited to self. It is a process of sliding back into an old pattern of modulating the self, culminating in the action of using drugs again. The therapeutic task is to identify this process *before* the client is at the action phase, and to help the addict to identify it.

This chapter describes five common patterns of behavior leading to relapse. Following each description are clinical examples, presented in the context of the self-modulation model of recovery. These five patterns of relapse are:

- Type A: The addict emphasizes action over meaning and self-awareness and returns to addiction because of the sense of action it produces.

- Unfinished Business: The addict avoids some past behavior or unresolved issue and returns to the addiction pattern of contact as a result.

- Chronic Relapse: The addict stays in recovery only for a short period of time, barely moving into the first stage before returning to full-fledged addiction.

- Conditional Recovery: The addict returns to addiction because a preset condition ("I'll stay sober as long as . . .") is not met, making addiction seem like a justified response.

- Lonely Long-Term Recovery: The addict feels neglected and unappreciated by others, including family and other addicts in recovery, and returns to addiction with a sense that recovery is no longer worth the effort.

All these types of relapse are examples of the movement from the fuller contact process to a pattern of contact analogous to the sensation-action pattern of addiction. Some fundamental changes in contact functioning may never have occurred, or the relapsing addict may have reverted after some period—even many years—of fuller contact. Figure 7.1 illustrates this movement from fuller contact to the abortive cycle of sensation-action.

In the full contact cycle (shown on the left side of Figure 7.1), a person develops sensations into full awareness, takes focused actions based upon the emerging awareness, maintains contact, and assimilates and closes the contact experience. While no recovering addict

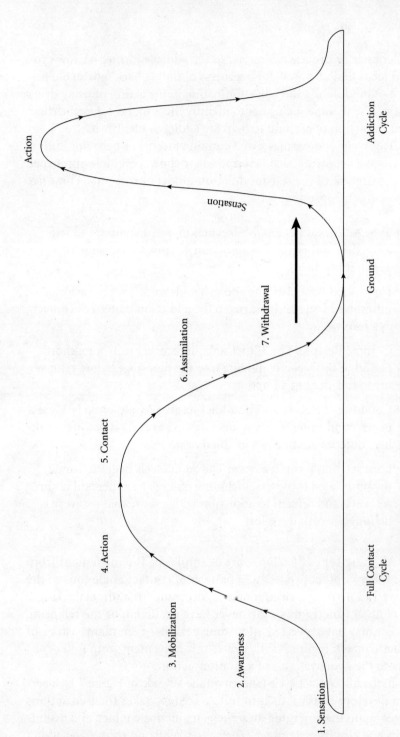

Figure 7.1. Relapse as Progressive Diminishing of Contact.

does this without interrupting some contact, the general pattern of contact for the recovering addict is similar to the full cycle. As the addict begins to move toward the flattened cycle (shown on the right in Figure 7.1), he or she is overstimulated. One response to this process is to desensitize or become depressed. Ironically, another common response to feeling overstimulated is to become more active, to do more and to do it more quickly. I have met many recovering addicts who have relapsed and who appear to be a whirl of activity, none of it focused. Often these people feel angry and cannot define the object of their anger. As a client once said: "I'm angry at everything and everyone. I don't know what about."

In relapse, the polarities of recovery are also unbalanced as the recovering addict begins to re-create the field of frustration, isolation, and pain that are the ground elements of using drugs. Addicts in relapse feel less known by others, have a narrow self-focus, and often derive most satisfaction from times of high activity. They overstimulate themselves and detach from environmental supports. Eventually, relapsing addicts experience their interpersonal field as a "do or die" situation; everything is crisis.

This behavior in recovery mirrors the addict's process of separation from others and his or her own feelings when using. In this process, the relapsing addict uses detached speech, physical desensitization, and avoidance instead of drugs for the same purposes that drugs formerly served. The addict may begin to feel different, unrelated to others. Often the addict becomes engaged in a constant level of activity: working, cleaning, worrying, or other forms of action. Relapsing addicts appear driven, much as they do when using drugs. Their emphasis is on action with little or no attention to awareness or closure.

The result of this activity is that relapsing addicts may be less aware of what they are experiencing, with all their focus on action. Twelve step programs often unintentionally support this level of activity. Their emphasis on doing may be appropriated by addicts as a new way to control self.

TYPE A RELAPSE PATTERN

In therapy with a recovering addict who has begun this pattern, I tend to draw attention to the sensations they are experiencing and focus less on action. Another approach I have used is to describe the addict's processes in detail, highlighting their pace and what may be missing (such as clearly defined figure, optional actions, and so on). Long-term recovering addicts seem less emotionally and cognitively available during the relapse process. This may not always be apparent, because they may attend twelve step meetings and speak in a kind of recovery jargon, explaining the change in their behavior if they are aware of it.

DAVID: "GETTING ON WITH MY LIFE"

David was clean for seven years when he adopted a course he described as "getting on with my life." He returned to college, bought a new car, and got a well-paying and stressful job—all within six months. Initially he seemed like himself, just busier. He began to skip AA meetings and to forget assignments or promises he'd made to others. He later described himself as having "tunnel vision," being able to see the road directly in front of him and little else. He became irritable and explained his irritation as the result of stress.

This process took over three years. He would go to bars, drinking club sodas, socializing with women who drank, never telling them that he wasn't drinking alcohol nor telling his recovering friends that he was going to bars. He began to live in two worlds, compartmentalizing his life. When his AA sponsor confronted him about spending so much time around alcohol and away from recovering people, David said that he didn't have time to talk but thanked his sponsor for the input.

David began drinking a little gin in his club soda. Within weeks he was using pills, and in three months had returned to injecting narcotics. David became hostile and abusive at work. He was eventually arrested for drunken driving and forced to return to AA meetings by the court.

David's "first drink" was the result of a process that had begun years earlier. It was not in his awareness to drink. What was figural was to get on with his life, a totally healthy goal. The problem was not with David's goal but rather with his process of attaining that goal, which led him to lose his job, quit college, and wreck his car. His process or style was to become less aware of himself by becoming increasingly active. He moved from sensation to sensation, acting on numerous figures at once. He said later that he was "trying to make up for all of my failures when I was using. I figured now was the time I could do that!" Embedded in this want was some nonacceptance of his past. That denial, in conjunction with his preference for a quick, desensitized pace, was the beginning of David's relapse.

David's story shows the difference between talking about self and talking from the full range of one's feelings and experiences. As recovering addicts relapse, they speak increasingly in a talk-about manner.

This is a kind of going though the motions of contact, which supports separation from one's feelings and experience. Eventually, by separating feelings and sensations from speech, addicts become less embedded in the interpersonal field.

PATRICK: MR. AA

Patrick had been active in AA since he'd stopped drinking. He was often asked to speak at meetings, and for fifteen years, he'd involved himself in helping other recovering addicts. After the first few years of recovery, Patrick's focus moved away from himself and almost exclusively into service to others. He often acknowledged this by saying "That's how I stay sober, not being self-centered."

Over time, Patrick's style of contact with others was based more on apparent commonalties than on any reflection or communication. His ongoing experience was one of confluence; he experienced few or no differences from others and very little awareness of himself. He spoke in a recovery jargon that seemed to assume an understanding with others, a kind of winking, "we know" manner of speech. Patrick had clearly moved through the first stage of recovery and remained in the early second stage. He had certainly mastered complementarity. His struggle was to fully experience the boundary between himself and others, filled with differences and new experiences. Instead, he maintained himself at a fixed state with little variation in external feelings. This process was the beginning of Patrick's relapse and the same as his pattern of alcohol use. Instead of maintaining himself through the drug, he did so by avoiding any internal changes, which he accomplished by separating himself from his sensations through thinking.

Eventually, Patrick became so busy with the program that he stopped attending to himself. He rarely described any difficulty to others. When he began to experience health problems, Patrick redoubled his level of activity. He had a minor heart attack and began to abuse prescribed medication in the weeks following surgery. His response when other alcoholics confronted him about this was "I'm an alcoholic, not a drug addict. I don't need to worry about drugs." It was only when Patrick began to drink again that he was willing to acknowledge the long process of relapse that had culminated in a return to alcohol.

I was consulted by a friend of Patrick's who asked me for suggestions in supporting Patrick. My recommendation was to have a meeting with Patrick and a few of his AA friends to talk with him about what he had done. My intention was to enhance Patrick's awareness of what he might do differently, and how his behavior affected others. I did this in conjunction with another therapist, and it helped Patrick to talk more freely about his shame over using again and also to hear from others about his relationship to them.

Neither David nor Patrick progressed through third-stage recovery. Patrick never developed interpersonal competency or allowed himself to experience the variety of contactful boundaries with others. He did not differentiate nor fully contact with others, but settled into an "as if" form of confluence. Others did not know his experience. David became so focused on where he was going that he lost awareness of where he'd been and neglected his present relationships. Both of these relapses were characterized by a loss of awareness based in the focus on action, which re-created the addiction pattern of contact through high activity. The other commonality in the two cases is the decrease in or loss of interpersonal contact.

UNFINISHED BUSINESS

In Gestalt therapy, the principle of unfinished business describes the persistent and natural process of our need for closure or resolution of experiences. We always have unfinished business, as not all situations can be fully resolved. For recovering addicts, unresolved personal and interpersonal issues can lead to a return to using drugs. This occurs when the unfinished business—a memory, for example, or a question of sexual orientation—persists in the addict's awareness and the addict needs to manage the feeling caused by that memory or question. Because this pattern can lead to drug use, AA and NA focus considerably on finishing up with past behavior. The following case is an example of the effect of unfinished business in the relapse of an addict.

ALICE: CHRONIC SHYNESS

Alice was abstinent for over ten years. She attended AA meetings on a regular basis and spoke the language of the program. But Alice had never dealt with her intense fear of people and in particular her fear of meeting them for the first time. She would enter meetings and immediately sit in the back of the room. If others approached her, she would smile and shake their hands. She didn't initiate conversations except on rare occasions with people she already knew. She would often attend small meetings—but never let herself get into small groups. She was able to work out of her home and maintained the majority of her contact with others by phone. Alice refused to enter therapy at the suggestion of her AA sponsor and friends because "the program gives me everything I need."

After Alice became a regular at certain meetings, she was less anxious about the interpersonal contact she might experience in that setting. Being a voracious reader, Alice devoured the literature of AA and could quote it chapter and verse. Her life improved when she stopped drinking, and she was able to diminish her fear of others.

Eventually, however, Alice could no longer work out of her home; she went to work in a large office setting with numerous fellow employees. Alice would become anxious in this situation and "highly nervous." She felt overwhelmed by her daily experience and gradually stopped attending meetings so she could recoup from the day. One evening, Alice stopped at a liquor store and bought a bottle on the way home from work. She didn't drink—but felt "safer" knowing she had the bottle with her. Alice experienced increasing difficulty facing people at work and avoided tasks that forced her to have contact with others. This pattern caused her performance to suffer and prompted the concern of her fellow employees. She was confronted about this by her supervisor, and when she missed days due to her fears, Alice was offered an option: seek treatment or lose her job. Alice made an appointment the next day.

The initial focus of my work with Alice was to help her examine what had led up to her process of relapsing and almost drinking. What she became aware of was her pattern of social avoidance. In her recovery, she had never moved beyond the narrow circle of her safety, and had not developed ways of making herself feel safer. In therapy, she discussed her fears and how alcohol helped her feel safe, "like a warm blanket."

Alice returned to AA meetings and continued in therapy. The continuing focus of our work was on helping her resolve or work through her fears of others. This led her to remember her childhood fear of large groups, which began at the time her parents were divorcing. Through visualizations of being in these large groups, Alice experienced how frightened she'd been as a child. She followed through on this individual work by joining a therapy group where she developed and practiced self-grounding and staying in contact with the individual group members rather than seeing them as a mass, as she'd seen groups as a child. In therapy, Alice began to work through the tasks of second-stage recovery, particularly of tolerating contact with others and of beginning to define her boundary, or sense of self, in relation to others.

In both Alice's and David's experiences, return to the addiction cycle developed long before the actual return to drinking. Neither David nor Alice experienced thoughts or even secret fantasies about taking a drink; that was neither's intention. Both David and Alice had unresolved or unfinished business they hadn't worked through in recovery. For David, it was his feelings of being a failure; for Alice, it was her phobic aversion to others. They each entered recovery and eventually became stuck in an habituated pattern, without exploring the important next ante. These changes were not initially observable from a behavioral perspective; both these clients attended meetings for years and appeared to be functioning in their lives. But if we look

at their process from a self-modulation perspective, they were shrinking or narrowing their interactions with others and returning to the
contact style, moving from sensation to action with minimal awareness.

CHRONIC RELAPSE

One of the most common patterns of relapse is when the recovering
addict remains abstinent and in recovery for short periods of time,
only to return to using drugs again and again. This is the form of
relapse that counselors and therapists see in outpatient addiction centers and detoxification units. The period of time between uses of the
drug varies from a few weeks to as much as a year. What I have found
to be consistent is that the relapsing addict gets to a similar time
period or stage of recovery after each relapse, and then returns to
using. Many of us who have worked with these clients have felt frustrated and confused by this process. I can think of many times when
I wondered what I had missed.

One image of this frustrating experience is of a clinician in a super-
vision session literally scratching his head and saying "I don't know."
Sometimes, as clinicians, we find solace, as do AA and NA members, in
coming up with an explanation for the addict's relapse: "He never
accepted his powerlessness . . . she isn't done with drinking yet. . . . "
Such postmortems may be helpful in explaining, but offer little direction for working with relapse.

What is apparent to me is that the chronic relapsing addict has
established a cycle that includes using drugs, abstinence, and using
drugs again. If the addict continues to relapse, then we need to address
this cycle in therapy. How is this cycle functional for this client? Is the
client's goal ever recovery, or only a temporary abstinence or reprieve
from the strain of using drugs? What does the chronically relapsing
addict learn during abstinence and each succeeding relapse? How does
continuing to work with this person in therapy reinforce or make this
pattern normative? These are some questions I have found useful to
ask myself and any relapsing client in order to address the pattern of
chronic relapse as a self-modulation.

TONI: "WHEN THINGS GET BORING, I'LL START USING AGAIN"

Toni was treated in detoxification units over ten times in three years. Each time she
entered treatment, she had been using crack cocaine and alcohol. By the time she made
an appointment to see me, she had virtually given up on anything different from her
pattern of a few weeks' abstinence before returning to using again.

The first question I asked Toni was whether she thought she was an addict. The second was what she liked about her pattern of using and getting abstinent. She said she was sure she was an addict. Her initial reaction to my second question was surprise. She said she was confused and that everyone had always told her it was "the disease" that made her get high.

I must have smiled when she said this because she looked angry and said, "You're not taking me seriously." I replied that I wanted to take her seriously but had difficulty with the whole idea that "it" made her get high. We talked for a while about this belief that it was something outside that was choosing her life. I suggested an experiment that might help her experience herself as the actor in her life. I suggested that she act out the part of *addiction*—that she role-play the "it" that made her do things.

The result of this experiment was startling. Instead of being confused, Toni seemed clear and directive. She stood up on a chair and said: "I'll use for a while. Then when I feel sick, I'll stop using, rest up, and when things get boring, I'll start using again. This way I can stay fresh when I get high. I have a couple more years of doing this."

When Toni finished, I asked her how she experienced herself. She said that she felt strong and that was so different from how she had ever felt before after relapsing. At these other times, she had felt apologetic and guilty. What amazed her about the role-play was the way she was "doing this because there are things I like about my way of life."

Toni and I agreed that she would not make another therapy appointment unless she decided to do so, that we would not assume her choice. This felt like a risk for me—I knew that she might go use again, and she did do so once more. But after that return to drugs she called me up and said, "I'm ready to stop doing this shit to myself . . . I want to come to therapy and meetings." We made an appointment for the following week.

This scenario with Toni illustrates the difference between the addict and therapist acting as if the relapsing client is a helpless victim of some external process and the addict and therapist attending to the addict's relapse as a form of self-modulation. Toni is an example of how recovery and avoiding relapse is based upon the addict's owning his or her behavior and taking responsibility whether to use again or stop the pattern. As long as she and her therapists treated her relapse as part of an epidemiological event, Toni's behavior and her choices remained external.

CONDITIONAL RECOVERY RELAPSE

I am describing this type of relapse as conditional because the recovering addict has placed some conditions on his or her recovery. These conditions might be "I'll stay sober as long as I don't suffer more than I did when using." Or "I don't know if I can not use if my husband dies."

Another kind of condition is the reservation some addicts have about returning to old drinking buddies, neighborhoods, or the possibility of returning to using a different drug. The danger of returning to another drug should be obvious. The problem of returning to the old people or places may not be clear for clinicians less familiar with the context of addiction. For the addicts, the entire milieu in which they used drugs is highly evocative of the act of using. Imagine the first four notes of a piece of music—say, Beethoven's Fifth Symphony: "da da da dum!" Try not humming the fourth note. We feel compelled to resolve the phrase. It seems natural and necessary. For addicts, being around people they have used with in the same scenario is like that musical phrase. Finishing it by getting high seems natural, the full phrase. The following case study is an example of a very talented and bright recovering addict who relapsed based upon conditions.

JAMAL: CHAMELEON MAN

Jamal stopped using drugs when he was twenty-three. He was forced into treatment by a series of arrests. He had grown up in a middle-class African American family, attended a college near his home, and moved into student teaching. This is what Jamal looked like to others or on paper—a solid, middle-class youth. In fact, he had begun using marijuana at fourteen, drinking soon after, and had graduated to heroin by the time he entered college. Jamal remained functional during his entire active addiction. He was able to maintain himself by his intelligence, quick wit, and good looks, and managed to scrape by numerous situations at school or with the police.

When Jamal entered rehabilitation treatment, he used these same skills. His treatment center was modeled on Synanon. Its method of treatment used confrontation in large groups and intense interactive therapeutic techniques intended to break down the defenses of the addicts in treatment. This methodology, more common in the 1960s and 1970s than it is now, is intended to deal with the characterological aspects of addicts (and alcoholics). Jamal's pattern of maintaining and adapting himself to his environment was quickly noticed by the residents and staff of the center. He was dubbed Chameleon, in reference to his ability to blend in with the environment. I was working at this center when Jamal entered treatment. I had few interactions with him, but I was able to see him in the larger community. It was at this level of system that Jamal and other residents were required to make announcements to the community of their particular game. This ritual was intended to make the community aware of whatever issues were the focus of each addict's individual treatment. The repetition of the statement also affected the person making the statement. Jamal's statement was "I am a chameleon and you can't see who I really am!" He would say this ten times a day to the whole community. Of course, the entire community became aware of Jamal. They eventually became irritated with him and began to focus on the way he behaved.

As I watched these interactions, I was most interested in Jamal's face when he made the statements. He sometimes would tighten up his face and almost appear to push out the words. Often he wouldn't look at anyone when he spoke. It was as if he were speaking into a vacuum. When community members confronted Jamal, he looked impassive, eyes blank and focused beyond the speaker. I sat down with Jamal after one of these interactions and asked him what it was like for him. He looked at me almost as a curiosity and said, "It's fine, I can do this all the time." I told Jamal that was exactly what concerned me about him. I wondered *how* he was able to do this all the time. He looked away from me and began talking to someone else.

Jamal left the treatment center and remained abstinent for three years. Because of his ability to articulate and his college education, he was offered a job as an addictions counselor. This fit Jamal's pattern of focusing more on helping or intervening with others than on attending to self. He was glib and impressed his supervisors with his appearance, an old pattern with Jamal. Within a year, Jamal was promoted to greater responsibility and worked more independently. He had returned to his old familiar pattern of *answer man:* a person who knew what to say to others and how to direct them to get help. In fact, Jamal was quite helpful to others and helped many people get off drugs and alcohol. The disadvantage of this pattern is that Jamal was more aware of others than of himself and perceived himself as beyond using again.

In his sixth year of sobriety, Jamal began to visit his old neighborhood again, to "see how things were and maybe help any old friends." Ironically, the result of the first of these visits was for Jamal to see how well off he was compared with people who were still using drugs. Like many primary drug addicts, Jamal had a reservation about drinking alcohol. After six and a half years of sobriety, Jamal had his first glass of wine during dinner with a woman who had no idea he was an addict. He felt the warmth of the alcohol in his body and nothing else happened. He decided that he would not drink any more that night. However, over time Jamal began drinking more and more wine with his meals and even buying a bottle to take home with him.

Eventually, Jamal returned to using, first marijuana and then heroin. He would show up late for work or sometimes not at all. He was able to not feel any contradiction in helping others stop using drugs while he was injecting heroin, a continuation of his lifelong pattern of separating his own experience from that of others. He was able to see clearly outside of himself but remained unaware of the contradictions in his own behavior. Because of his lateness and missed days, Jamal was fired from his job. The same week, the woman he had been involved with found him with a needle in his arm, passed out in his bedroom. She was shocked and called an ambulance. Jamal was not in any immediate danger: he had simply passed out. Nonetheless, he was taken to a detoxification center (where he had worked only three weeks before) and referred to the relapse treatment unit.

A major emphasis of Jamal's treatment was on the contradictory lifestyle that he had followed most of his life. Jamal could see and help others, yet he was impervious to any help or input from others. For the first time in years, Jamal showed some anger, storming out of a group therapy session after he was confronted by the leader and group members about this pattern. His anger sensitized Jamal so much that he told everyone in the facility how incompetent he thought they were compared to him.

I was working as a consultant to this unit and recognized Jamal one day when he burst out of a room in anger. He asked me if we could talk and he told me the story of his relapse. When he finished, Jamal said, "Well, I suppose you're not surprised." I told Jamal I was more relieved that he was alive and glad to hear him expressing his anger. We agreed to talk if he needed to during his treatment.

The treatment staff supported Jamal in his angry outburst, encouraging him to "get it out," with the awareness that he was finally expressing himself emotionally. When he was done, the staff asked Jamal how he was feeling. He responded that he could feel himself throughout his whole body, and he felt angry and sick. The importance of this interaction is that Jamal began to experience himself rather than to focus only on what others wanted or did. The paradox is that by supporting his anger toward others, he was able to more fully experience himself. Jamal's contact style was one of superficial or minimal sensitization; he could not allow himself to feel too much. One result of this process was that he (and others) experienced himself through his persona or "as if" presentation. Jamal came across as if things didn't bother him, as if he had no doubts and was always in control. This left him isolated and feeling different from others. His choice of desensitizing drugs (alcohol, heroin, marijuana) further supported this pattern of obscuring sensation.

Following treatment, Jamal returned to twelve step meetings (both AA and NA) and took what he called a "regular job," working in a restaurant. He decided it was essential to not return to a position that separated him from his peers. This was important because Jamal tended to isolate himself and to end up feeling impervious and untouchable. For him, the crucial stage was connecting and experiencing his similarity to others. He became involved in a group of recovering African American men, where he eventually felt integrated. I had suggested this group to him because of my sense that some of his experience of being different was based in cultural differences. He agreed with this interpretation and later reported to me that he was "part of a group."

Working with Jamal (and other clients) has made me aware of the limitation of traditional therapeutic alliances. In a sense, our work was not enough for Jamal; he needed to reenter *his* African American community as a sober man. His chameleonlike behavior is not unusual for a minority member in a system dominated by a majority (as was the treatment facility and as are present fields of psychology, counseling, and social work). To fully own his recovery and change, Jamal needed to experience himself in the context of other recovering African Americans.

Jamal is also an example of an addict who relapsed after some period of abstinence. The common question can be posed: How did this happen? *If it did not simply occur, then he made some choices about his thoughts and behaviors.* The language that we use about addiction reveals our bias. Like many addicts who use after some period of abstinence, Jamal did some things and did not do others. He chose to drink coffee and soft drinks in bars, and he associated with familiar people who did not know he was an addict and with people who used alcohol and drugs. He created the perfect scenario for drinking: anonymity and a supportive environment for drug use. By associating himself with people who did not know about him, Jamal had to rely exclusively on his own resources to not use. He had not integrated the second stage of recovery. He had reservations about drinking alcohol and did not engage others to support him in retroflecting the action of using.

LONELY LONG-TERM RECOVERY

Many long-term recovering addicts end up feeling isolated and disconnected after years of recovery. Not unlike elderly relatives, many of their peers have passed on or returned to using drugs. The result is a sense of difference and disconnection from the support system.

ED: UNRECOGNIZED AND ANGRY

After ten years of recovery, Ed stopped attending meetings because "they don't appreciate everything that I've done." He pointed to having started numerous meetings, and to making the coffee and cleaning up every week for five years. When the AA group wanted to celebrate his tenth anniversary, Ed refused to attend. He was unable to let others appreciate or recognize him. His explanation was that they were only going through the motions now and should have acknowledged him before. He was angry and bitter, but mostly hurt by what he perceived to be a lack of recognition. His focus was exclusively on others and how they *treated him.*

The root of all this was an incident in which a newcomer to the meeting forgot Ed's name and his ninth anniversary when making announcements. I asked Ed to imagine he was a camera on wheels and that he could move back and forth to experiment with different perspectives of himself and the group. When he pulled back he saw "the whole scene . . . what they were trying to do by acknowledging my anniversary . . . how I look hurt and am turning away while they are talking to me. I can see how hurt I am and how the group seems not to notice. They are assuming I'm fine because I've been sober for ten years. I can see myself getting angry." Ed was able to identify his hurt and eventually to return to the meeting. He was willing to talk about this experience in therapy.

Not all recovering addicts have the support system of therapy. If unexamined, their process becomes similar to drinking behavior, except without the drug or drink, a process referred to as a *dry drunk*. The recovering addict's process begins to resemble the shortened cycle as described in Chapter Two, with a rapid movement from sensation to habitual action, in this case, withdrawal from others and little or no awareness of self. This process is what Gorski and Miller describe as one stage of the relapse into drinking or using drugs.

<hr>

These case examples show the different paths by which addicts in some form of recovery return to active addiction. In each person's story is the pattern of some disconnection or estrangement from others. As happens throughout their addiction, these relapsing addicts first modulate their own self-awareness, emphasizing action and desensitization over reflection and sensory awareness. They all stopped moving though the stages of recovery and reverted to their earlier behaviors of barely managing their own boundaries.

The therapeutic approaches I have described are based in a very experiential field and emphasize heightening addicts' awareness of themselves and their behavior. This is both the characteristic approach of Gestalt therapy and an appropriate approach for relapsing addicts, who by nature are cut off from their experience, often intellectualizing about themselves. These interventions are also designed to encourage addicts (for example, Toni) to take responsibility for their behavior in either heading toward the drug or toward contact with self and others.

Relapse occurs in long-term recovery in part due to the underdeveloped aspects of self and self-support, as well as the assumption that simply not drinking or not using is enough. Yet not drinking or using is merely sobriety. *Recovery* is the increasingly personal process of expanding and developing self in relation to others. Ironically, relapse may be the learning the recovering addict needs, as difficult as that may be for us as clinicians to tolerate. Patrick probably wouldn't have been able to hear from others what he learned by relapsing. The risk, of course, is that relapse may be lengthy and damaging or even fatal rather than educational. Many addicts do not return from relapse.

This chapter has focused on the varieties of relapses during recovery. Relapse is a significant but not exclusive clinical issue in working with recovering addicts. The next chapter focuses on individual differences among recovering addicts and the effect these differences have on recovery and possible clinical interventions. The complexities of individual differences in recovering addicts present another clinical challenge.

Recommended Reading

Gorski, T., & Miller, M. (1986). *Staying sober: A guide for relapse prevention.* Independence, MO: Herald House.

CHAPTER EIGHT

Individual Differences

—*m*— Current addiction treatment tends to emphasize the common characteristics among addicts. The old adage, "All addicts are the same, addiction is the same" remains a dictum of treatment centers and twelve step programs. The perceived accuracy of these statements derives from the way addicts appear to share some common feelings (perhaps in more extreme form than found among the general population) such as guilt and insecurity, a common tendency toward overstimulation or even hyperactivity, and compulsive use of drugs.

Addicts do, however, vary a great deal, in terms of both their personal development and their sociocultural and gender experiences outside their addiction. For example, consider a seventeen-year-old addict entering treatment after using drugs since the age of thirteen. Her ability to move in the world and make contact with others as well as her sense of identity will be reduced by her intoxication and unfinished contact experiences. While all life experiences are significant, the experiences of adolescence are formative and shape the way we interact socially and our sense of confidence. This kind of shaping of the ground will influence the way this young woman interacts in her adult life. She will not merely "get off drugs" and pick up with her peers. In addition to the tasks of recovery already discussed, recovery for her will include reexperiencing herself relationally without the drug and needing to develop new ways of dealing with her own changing body, her competency, and how the world experiences her.

By contrast, a forty-five-year-old woman stockbroker who began drinking at age thirty-two is in a very different situation. She went through college and earned an MBA before alcoholism became a factor in her life. Although her drinking may have cost her personally and professionally, she has had an experience of initiating, leading, and influencing people. Her identity will be affected by her drinking—but she has some developed social competencies to draw from in recovery. She appears smooth and is an excellent problem solver. Her difficulty is in allowing others to support her. Treatment for her may focus on seeing the value of sharing control with others.

Just as the maxim "all addicts are the same" fails to provide much assistance to a therapist faced with women like the two described here, it tends to fall short in practice with each unique individual working through the stages of recovery. Each addict has his or her own level and manner of personality organization, psychological and cognitive development, age, gender, and contextual grounds of culture and race. These differences may not necessitate different kinds of treatment, but can be guides for therapists in understanding the contextual issues of recovery. They are important in that they present different grounds out of which the figures of drug and alcohol use emerge. Moreover, the differences among addicts become more important in the course of recovery. The tasks of recovery tend to differ among addicts after the early stages.

DIFFERENCES IN PERSONALITY ORGANIZATION

One of the ongoing assumptions of the addiction treatment and recovery community is the so-called addictive personality. Unfortunately, research does not support the idea that there is any personality that all addicts share. Jerome Levin and others have come to this conclusion through examining and reviewing the various studies and clinical examples.

As I have described addicts, they do share certain styles of contact and behavior, ranging from intolerance of sensation to spiritual hunger or yearning. But addiction is a contact style rather than a personality, a style that is related to but only part of the whole ground that is personality. Gary Yontef describes a number of aspects of personality, all consistent with the idea of personality as process. These aspects include ongoing contact functions and capabilities that shape the way in which the person understands, experiences, and potentially integrates contact with others.

The other distinction I find useful is that of primary and secondary addiction. In *primary* alcoholism (or addiction), there is no identifiable preexisting psychological condition. Primary addicts tend to recover via the process described in the stages of recovery. Their capacities for contact return or are developed in a smooth pattern. Their movement through the stages depends on their willingness to experiment and their environmental support systems.

The term *secondary addict* refers to a person who experienced some preexisting emotional or cognitive disorder prior to abuse and dependency on drugs or alcohol. The most common of these preexisting or coexisting conditions are three personality disorders: borderline, narcissistic, and antisocial. With such clients, the danger of their progression through addiction is just as potentially lethal as with primary addicts. If they are truly addicted, their addiction is not a symptom of their personality but a pattern coexisting with their personality. In fact, these clients, referred to by Denis Daley, Howard Moss, and Frances Campbell as exhibiting *dual disorders,* may use alcohol and drugs as a form of medication to lessen their discomfort or to support their need for stimulation or desensitization. As with other addicts, what begins as a useful self-modulation eventually becomes difficult and later impossible to control.

My experience has been that helping such clients stop drinking or getting high does not restore them to better interpersonal relationships. One of the challenges for these clients occurs in the complementarity task of second stage recovery. They generally have difficulty living in an equal and shared field of contact. Nor does mere abstinence improve their ability to tolerate contact. In fact, the persistence of certain behaviors and difficulties in recovery can be diagnostic of a pervasive personality disorder. In many cases, the absence of drugs coincides with more intense feelings, thoughts, and patterns of interaction.

To distinguish these behaviors from normal recovery, I will present some descriptions and examples. This is important because, as

Daley, Moss, and Campbell point out, many of the traits of personality disorders exist in the general population, but to a lesser degree than among addicts.

Borderline Addict

The difficulty for this type of client emerges after some period of recovery, although a thorough history can identify some early relationship and self-identity patterns of difficulty. Many addicts behave in the intense and highly reactive patterns we associate with borderline personality when they are actively using. Therefore, some period of abstinence is necessary to determine if an addict is truly a borderline personality.

Borderline personality addicts have extreme difficulty in interpersonal relationships. According to Elinor Greenberg, borderline clients shift between an idealistic fusion with others and anger, fear of abandonment, and rage-filled attempts to annihilate previously valued significant others. Such addicts usually struggle with being members of any system, group, or program, tending to feel rejected by others and also demanding attention and some kind of fusion or boundary merger with others. Because of this demand for an idealized other, the borderline addict is often disappointed and angry. For such addicts, twelve step meetings and programs are potential opportunities for fusion. This is usually the same experience that they create in therapy or treatment. The struggle for borderline is the self in relation; the mutual give and take that cocreates a shared boundary between people in everyday life.

Borderline personalities tend to divide others into good and bad people from what is believed to be a projection of their own internal split. For the borderline addict, abstinence is often not as figural as finding "good" people who understand them. The problem with this is twofold: that the very same individuals often by some oversight or lack of attention to the borderline become "bad" people; and that the borderline client doesn't get to experience his or own internal sense of goodness and badness. Instead, he or she projects the internal experience onto others. In that process, the borderline addict usually irritates or overwhelms his or her support system in recovery. The stage of connecting to a group is extremely difficult for these clients. Their need for both fusion and differentiation may so dominate the field that they become fringe to their recovery programs. If they are in individual therapy, this then becomes the major focus of their lives and can also result in another disappointment. It is easy for the therapist and client to become totally embroiled and lose focus on the client's recovery from addiction.

Celia, a client who came to "interview" me as a potential therapist, serves as an example of this process. She had been in therapy many times before (more than ten) and had never found a therapist who understood her. Recently, she had gotten into a series of conflicts in her home AA group that all seemed to center on her feeling of not getting enough support from others. She was angry and blaming everyone for failing to meet her needs. Her reason for coming to see me was that I might understand her. I told her that I didn't know what I might do that was different from everyone else and that I suspected I would eventually disappoint her. She was furious and screamed at me that I was telling her it was all her fault. We talked about this for some time. I said that I believed we are all responsible for our interactions, as I was taking responsibility for ours at that moment. I further described that if I acted as if I could do something for her that no one else could, I would be misleading her.

In working with Celia, I was attending to the parameters of our relationship. I did this because that was her focus and main struggle outside of therapy. Believing that we would probably go down the road of her other relationships, I focused the contract of our work on her expectations and what I believed I could and would do. I did not want to promise her that I would be "good" and meet all her expectations. My statement of limitations was difficult for her to tolerate and it evoked her internal absolutism. We were able to explore how this very process was pervasive in all of her relationships.

These conflicts are typical for borderline clients. What is significant about them is that they may be triggers or justifications for using drugs again. Because of this potential, it is important for the therapist to hold an awareness of the dual struggle of borderline addicts. Both processes must be attended to in the therapy: recovery from addiction does not heal the borderline split, nor vice versa. Recovery programs often offer a degree of intimacy for which borderline addicts yearn. Therapy is most helpful when the field is broad enough to allow for the full perspective of both personality disorder and addiction. I have found it helpful, in working with borderline addicts, to carry this awareness with me.

Narcissistic Addict

For some theorists, addiction and narcissism have become synonymous terms. Alcoholics have long been considered to have narcissistic traits. In fact, the emphasis of the twelve step programs is on decreasing egoism and on movement away from self-centeredness to other-focus. Clearly, the cofounder of Alcoholics Anonymous, Bill Wilson, had strong narcissistic characteristics.

But narcissistic personality disorder is more than being self-centered and sensitive to criticism. Narcissistic addicts also have a limited capacity for contact with others; they are unaware of their environment as being different from them. Narcissistic addicts often appear very capable. Because of this they can be put into positions of leadership in twelve step programs, positions they can only handle from their own perspective and feelings. Because of their capacity to look good, they are sometimes not noticed in addiction treatment programs where the emphasis is on the limited goals of increasingly shorter treatment and education to the so-called disease.

One difficulty for narcissistic addicts is to admit their limitations. With addiction, this limitation is powerlessness, the inability to control either the drug or one's behavior when intoxicated. The second limitation faced by the narcissistic addict is the need for environmental support such as twelve step groups or help from others. As I write this, I am remembering Joe, a narcissistic addict who was in a treatment facility where I worked. No matter what was said to him, his immediate answer always began with "I know." He could not let himself appear to learn anything new for fear he would look stupid. His need to appear all-knowing pervaded all his interactions. This man's struggle was treated as one of denial of his addiction.

I spent some time working with Joe during his treatment. As with other addicts, Joe's challenge was to perceive himself as an equal in a world of others. To do that, he had to run the risk of humiliation and also reach out to experience others. I asked Joe what he thought others might know and what he knew. His response was initially quick, referring to something else that he knew but avoiding answering my question. I repeated the question twice and he finally looked at me. He answered that either he or others had to know something more. I wondered if he could know something different from what I knew, and that we could be equal. His face reddened and he looked away from me. I was struck by his aversion to my offer that we could actually complement each other. This was unthinkable for him. My style of intervention with him was nonconfrontational and curious, designed to appeal to his understanding. But I guided him into a shadow land that he rarely let himself experience, the unknown. Later, Joe wanted to know what I knew but wasn't telling him, and we worked with his interest in me and his fear of not knowing everything.

Ironically, narcissistic personalities can do well in twelve step programs if they are able to stop drinking. These programs can offer a forum for them to discuss their favorite subject: themselves. This is also true for narcissistic addicts in individual therapy, unless the therapist attends to therapy as a two-person system. Otherwise, the narcissistic addict continues to focus on self in a shallow self-presenting manner while the therapist listens and reflects. While this scenario may seem a little exaggerated, in lesser extremes it is often what occurs for narcissistic addicts. I remember a comment Joe Melnick, a Gestalt trainer, made in a workshop: "The goal of therapy with narcissists is to get them interested in the therapist." With narcissistic addicts, this is also my experience, yet I would broaden this goal to "getting them interested in *anyone other than themselves.*"

In relation to the process of recovery, the narcissistic addict will need more attention paid to the middle stages of recovery, those that focus on interpersonal relationships. The difficulty in early recovery will be one of admitting limitation, but only later will the emptiness of internal experience emerge in interpersonal situations. Without developing contactful interpersonal relationships during later stages of recovery, moving to transpersonal will seem easy for the narcissistic addict. But often this will be a mirror of their own isolated internal image rather than grounded in others.

Antisocial Addict

The effectiveness of Gestalt therapy relies on a client's excitement and anxiety to develop the work. In a sense, we are interested in and attend to discomfort and impasses and similar difficult matters. But what if there is minimal discomfort with the exception of anger and the discomfort of hunger or sexual need? What if there is little or no warmth, attachment, or interest in others, even when hurt? These are some of the characteristics of antisocial personality disorder, along with impulsiveness, lack of remorse, deceitfulness, and irritability. According to

Daly, Moss, and Campbell, this is the most common personality disorder among alcoholics. I have worked with dozens of antisocial addicts in both institutional and private practice settings.

I have found that many addicts appear antisocial while they are using; in fact, many commit felonies and appear untouched by the pain of others. Early life histories are important for making this diagnosis. The other element is to reevaluate these clients after six months, a year, and five years of recovery

Contact with others and groups is usually of no concern to antisocial addicts. They are not interested in fellowship or intimacy even though they may say these words. Recovery usually takes on a utilitarian frame, but the antisocial addict has low tolerance for any prolonged contact with others. They notoriously resent authority unless they are the ones in that position. My experience of working with these clients is that the best approach is a practical one. In early recovery, don't bother with how they feel about what they did. The approach could be framed like this: "*Using drugs cost me time, hurt my body. Using drugs causes me problems. What do I have to do to not use drugs?*"

For antisocial addicts, this level of development is how they organize the field. The antisocial addict is profoundly desensitized without using drugs. In recovery, this pattern of desensitization does not end with abstinence. Any therapy approach focusing on sensitizing the antisocial addict will probably be unsuccessful or take years to show some fruition. Antisocial addicts may not move through later stages of recovery. If they do and are capable of this work, it is an enormous struggle for the client and therapist. The work involves repeated struggle through layers of desensitization and contempt. Here is a case example to illustrate this struggle.

SCOTT

Scott was a thirty-four-year-old man who had spent five years in prison for what he called a "phony" drug charge. He'd stopped using drugs or alcohol in prison and had joined NA. Since his release, he'd returned to college and graduate school, eventually earning a law degree. In his law practice, he had been accused of some ethical violation, and this time he was actually innocent.

When he called me for an appointment, I was struck by how unemotional he sounded. During this initial appointment, Scott seemed impassive as he told me how he was going to blow up the office of the man he believed had accused him. As we talked, I was shocked by his repeated mention of bodily damage to others with no apparent emotion. I asked him about this and he laughed, "That's the way it is . . . they do me . . . I do them." The only way that Scott could back off from his violent fantasies was when I pointed out how much he might lose (law practice, BMW, beautiful house) and suggested that he could take this man to court. In a sense, I suggested that Scott use the legal process as an aggressive outlet, not an uncommon practice in our society. Scott decided that I was a "useful" therapist and he made another appointment. At that time he brought a box of fresh pears. The gesture is a classic one in prison, a favor for a favor. I thought about this gift for a while and took the pears but said I had a question. My question was one that Scott and I pursued for two years as we struggled though his reconnection to society. I asked him if he was uncomfortable feeling like he owed me.

For Scott, as with other antisocial addicts, the give and take of interpersonal relationships was a novel experience. He could not tolerate the feeling of appreciation. He later reported that giving me the fruit was a way not to feel indebted. Before he could tolerate relationships where people were more than "useful," he needed to explore his numbness and rage. I was different enough for him to trust with his plans.

DIFFERENCES IN ENVIRONMENTAL SUPPORT IN RECOVERY

For addicts, environmental support is an important factor in moving through the stages of recovery. By environmental support, I am referring to everything in the field that is not the self. The common understanding of support is often that of exactly agreeing, mirroring, or being confluent. The Gestalt notion of support, derived from the work of Lore Perls, refers to that which is background, unaware but "indispensable *support* for the foreground function of contact." This support includes other people, ideas, groups, and physical supports such as meditation and exercise. The variation of degree and types of support can influence the relative need for support from the therapist or group. My experience is that most therapy and integration takes place between sessions, so support outside of the therapy sessions and twelve step meetings can help integrate the addict's changing field. While it is not necessary for an addict's family or partner to cooperate with his or her recovery, such immediate environmental support can be a large advantage.

My own experience of supporting recovering clients is to use myself in a number of ways. These range from witnessing the change to confronting obvious denial to sharing my own experience to remaining curious and interested about the struggle. Sometimes I have supported the addicts' own self-support by frustrating their attempts to make me an expert.

Addicts live much of their lives in isolation and tend to bear their experiences either by toughing it out or by having someone else take over. These two poles are another face of the theme of horizontality. Support is a middle mode where the environment and others are an interested but differentiated part of the field; the struggle is still the addict's. The richer that field, the more the addict is free to vary and experiment with new behaviors.

Environmental support can take many forms. When I work with addicts in different stages of recovery, I try to identify what supports they have for the work, both self-supports and environmental. Individual therapy can support self-development and many of the tasks described in the stages of recovery (development of sensation, developing retroflection, interpersonal competence, and the tasks of third-stage recovery).

My belief of the larger systems modes of therapy are that their effectiveness depends on the addict's development of the tasks of the first stage of recovery. To make use of the support of couples or family therapy, the recovering addict needs to be less immediately focused on managing self-boundary. This may take a few weeks or as long as a year for some recovering addicts. The use of group therapy can support all stages of recovery, with different emphasis at different stages. In first-stage recovery, educational and discussion groups seem to support the tasks of maintaining abstinence and developing inhibition to the drug. The task of developing sensations into awareness can be supported in group therapy that is experientially based.

Support in recovery is basically support for contact and development. Because the recovering addict's contact expands in recovery, the types of support will also broaden or change in recovery. Some groups or people that the recovering addict found useful in early recovery may not support changes in middle and later recovery. This is often a sore point among recovering addicts, who may feel left or rejected by the addict's change. It is often our role as therapists to help the client process these kinds of interaction. An example of this frequently occurs when a recovering addict moves into a different spiritual approach from others. I have worked with recovering clients who feel they have nothing in common with their former peers and need to develop new support systems. The challenge is for them to trust their own need while developing alternative supports.

GENDER DIFFERENCES

If recovery is a restoration of contact functioning and intertwined with psychological, social, and emotional development, then gender differences in recovery should be prevalent. Sheila Blume stresses the importance of low self-esteem and the need to confront feelings of individuality and dependency in women alcoholics.

My clinical experience supports both these themes, as well as the impact of gender social stereotypes on the way women addicts view their drug and alcohol use. The old introjects and judgments about "drinking like a lady" and the double standard of our culture about sexual behavior when intoxicated often help to create shame and self-contempt in women addicts.

In recovery, differences in development and developmental emphasis between women and men seem to show up. Along with these differences, the bias in our developmental theories toward differentiation as being more ideal than connection can lead to a type of discounting of the experiences and styles of women addicts. The self-modulation is an attempt to describe *recovery from addiction* as the development of the self in relation and *addiction* as the self in isolation. The dynamic tension between the self embedded in relation with others and individual identity is the emphasis of the second stage of recovery.

In my clinical experience, recovery is not a process of becoming increasingly autonomous; it is a dance between developing self and developing connection in larger fields of relatedness. To do this, women and men addicts may need to emphasize and develop different tasks in recovery. The primary struggle beyond abstinence and inhibition is the continued development of what Judith Jordan calls the "relational self."

It is also my experience that many women addicts struggle with and need to develop individuation and self-support, particularly in relation to men. This movement is not a separation from others, but rather a development of individual capacities while interconnected with others. In contrast, many men recovering from addiction do not have experience of attending to the maintenance, support, and emotional consistency of interconnectedness. Often male addicts have to develop these kinds of gluing behaviors, and are overly developed in individuation and autonomy. These are general statements—but they mostly hold true: female addicts often need to develop more internal strengths, while male addicts often need to develop in relation to others (family, group, primary partnership). This may certainly be related to socialization practices in our culture, which tend to emphasize these characteristics or even develop them along gender lines. The problem comes when, as clinicians, we value one of these ends of the polarity over the other.

Some examples may illustrate applications of this model to gender differences. The story of Agnes (in Chapter Five) shows us a person who developed social abilities and defined herself in relation to another (her husband). For her, the development of her own professional identity, separate from an other, was a significant development passage. While she was very involved with her grandchildren and as a mother figure to young women in AA, her development as an autonomous woman was crucial in her recovery.

In contrast, Mark (also in Chapter Five) was well developed in doing things on his own and had a clear professional identity. For him, the significant developments in recovery were in relation to others. What became salient for him as he moved into middle recovery was "fathering" a fatherless boy. While he remained active in his job, what was more significant for him was making a difference in someone else's life. These issues of balancing different aspects of self in relation were fundamental in both Agnes's and Mark's therapy and recovery.

Another key element in gender differences in therapy with recovering addicts is the differing experiences of being part of a dominant or subordinate group. Male recovering clients may be more socially empowered to express anger and differentiation, and even to challenge the therapist. Such behavior in therapy and life is not as socially supported for women. In working with female clients in the second stage of recovery on the tasks of boundary flexibility and redefinition, I always want to be aware of differences in the sense of empowerment, particularly in relation to my maleness. Frequently, the recovering woman addict's self-modulation needs to be understood in the context of our gender boundary. In this way, our therapy encounter will offer more choices grounded in her ongoing social context.

RACIAL AND ETHNIC DIFFERENCES

Differences in drug use among ethnic and racial groups seem to be contextual. That is, the ethnic context or system influences the type of drug used, the social behavior of addicts, and the cultural value and meaning of drug use and abstinence. Consequently, clients' ethnicity is an important part of their interpersonal field and the lens through which they see themselves and the world.

In working with recovering addicts, the client's ethnicity is an important part of the ground for us to attend to, especially if it is different from our own. As Gael Caution puts it, "To ignore a people's culture is to dismiss their value, beliefs, and assumptions about the universe." My manner of learning about a recovering client's culture is to be curious, both in my own training and with the client. I do not ask a client to teach me about his or her culture but rather remain attentive to what field of interrelatedness he or she lives in. My stance is also to be phenomenological and not to assume that because other clients are from the same culture that something true of them *is also true for this client.* My stance is to hold my awareness of culture while exploring this person. Assumptions about client cultural values and histories are another form of being out of contact with the fullness of this individual or group.

Addiction and Ethnicity

Clearly, individuals exist and understand themselves within systems of values, norms, and rituals. One of the most common rituals in many cultures is the use of alcohol or drugs. When an addict's behavior is aberrant or problematic, it is because he or she is in some way out of the norm of drinking or drug use. This behavior stands out from the rest of the system's order: hence, it is a *dis-order.* Many addicts, particularly primary alcoholics, have described not knowing what normal drinking is, because "Everyone I know drinks like me."

I remember working with Ray, a young Irish American man in treatment whose entire family drank regularly, if not daily. All of the men in his extended family were either in AA or frequently intoxicated. He could not imagine a social event without alcohol, probably because he had never attended one. Soon after he left treatment, while trying to remain sober, he visited his uncle. The uncle, while very fond of his nephew, offered Ray a beer three times after he described his attempt to stay sober.

This is an example of the interrelationship between the addict's attempt to maintain a boundary with drugs and the environment's lack of support. This newly sober alcoholic decided he could not "stay sober and be around my family." In this case, his own need was more important or figural for him than the pull of his family. In Gestalt language, we would describe his uncle and family as having a fixed, rigid boundary with regard to alcohol use. This is the first stage of recovery, the task of developing retroflections of the drug.

The importance of this example is to highlight the ethnic context of drinking or drug. Ray's uncle could not imagine getting together without having a "cold one." This is what the family had done for generations. There was nothing hostile in the offer of beer; it was an assumed behavior. The struggle for the recovering addict was, having made his abstinence his goal, to let his family loyalties become secondary.

A second example is Rose, a fortyish Jewish American woman whose extended family was religiously observant and professionally oriented. Drunkenness or excessive use of alcohol would result in ostracism from the whole family, but it was perfectly acceptable to use prescription medications. She became addicted to Valium prescribed by her psychiatrist. Her family did not perceive her to have a problem as long as she was seeing a professional and not visibly drunk. No one confronted her about her drug use. We might look at this example as *denial* of addiction by the family system. But the larger level of system, the ethnic or cultural level, reveals specific beliefs about what is disorder. For Rose and her family to examine her drug addiction, these norms had to be examined in a family intervention—after she nearly died from an overdose of Valium.

The effect of race and culture can be the ground for addicts to use. Modulating the effects of culture and racism can be accomplished through desensitization. In recovery, the addict confronts this experience without the modulating effects of the drug.

JUMPING OUT OF MY SKIN

Tom was a black man of twenty-seven who had been clean of heroin for three years. Every time he had to speak or appear in public, he felt like he was going to jump out of his skin. He had always felt like this, but learned as an adolescent that if he had a drink or smoked marijuana, "I wouldn't care what happened or what people thought of me." Over the years, he progressed to using heroin and other narcotics, and when intoxicated rarely felt anxious or self-conscious. It seemed clear that this was because he didn't feel rather than because he'd worked through these fears. When he became abstinent, Tom's fears and self-consciousness reemerged as enormous social discomfort. When he attended AA or NA meetings, he quickly found a seat so as to avoid the discomfort of being "looked at by the whole group."

Tom came to my office for an appointment on a Monday morning. As he talked about his current discomfort, he kept referring to using heroin: "I never had to worry about this shit when I was high." I looked at his chest moving quickly and shallowly with each breath. It was clear to me that Tom was mobilized and was more aware of wanting to stop his sensations than he was of what they were about. In Gestalt language, we might describe Tom as having energy around an unclear figure. I slowed myself down and paid attention to Tom's breathing, hearing his words "jumping out of my skin." I looked at my skin while I breathed and then looked at Tom's skin. The contrast stood out to me, his dark brown skin, my freckled and pinkish complexion. When I mentioned this to Tom, he looked at his arm and hands. I then said, "This is the skin you want to jump out of!"

Tom's breathing slowed down until his chest was filled with long rhythmic inhalations. He said, "People don't look at you the way they stare at me!" I agreed that this was probably true. I wondered if he felt like jumping out of his skin when *I* looked at his arm and hands. As he attended to his body sensations, he reported that he did feel the same nervousness and his breathing became tight and rapid.

I suggested to Tom, "Is it like I see your skin and not you?

"Yeah . . . you are white. Like the people on the city bus I rode as a kid . . . they all just stared at me but not at me . . . at my blackness . . . they looked disgusted and I couldn't get away from them." I suggested to Tom that he had found a way to get away from them, to get away from the feeling by using alcohol and drugs. He agreed and talked to me about his earliest use of drugs and how much better he felt riding the bus when he was high.

Tom and I developed a clear figure of his experience of being looked at by whites and his response of "jumping out of" or leaving his skin by using drugs. We went for a walk near my office and both paid attention to how people looked at us and how we felt. This session was rich with the differences in our experiences and Tom's sense of isolation and feeling of being the object of disgust. The focus of this work was not on Tom's past use of heroin or his recollection of how it was helpful to him. I clearly focused on developing the sensation that Tom modified by using heroin. I also took his words "jumping out of my skin" quite literally. I believed him and suggested that he believe himself.

These are basic premises of Gestalt therapy, attending to the development of sensations into feelings and attending to the obvious, literal experience, including the client's use of language as reflective of experience. In this example, the obvious, literal experience for Tom was his skin color and its contrast to mine. This approach stands in contrast to an analysis of the unconscious meaning of Tom's experience as a black man or to operating from some sociological assumptions about the issues for African Americans. By our focusing on Tom's theme of the difference in our skins, he was able to experience the discomfort he described in the moment. I was operating from the belief that Tom's nervousness was an indication of something significant in his field of awareness. In Gestalt therapy, we refer to this as *excitement* in the sense of rising energy. Tom's use of drugs had become an interruption of this excitement and nervousness that he could now tolerate experiencing and could now explore.

What is significant in this example is that Tom and I attended to his feelings instead of to his drug use. By our attention to this part of Tom's experience, he was able to work through his *present* discomfort. If he had used drugs, his feelings of discomfort would have been diminished out of his awareness. He was able to explore his relationship or boundary with others. If he had used the drug, his relationship would have been with the drug, what J. Richard White called being "enmeshed with the drug." In this situation, Tom was able to develop a figure other than the drug itself.

Culturally Divergent Recovery

At one time, there were few supports among certain ethnic groups for recovering addicts. AA and NA meetings had not proliferated across the ethnic and social spectrum. This is no longer the case, and treatment services as well as self-help groups are virtually everywhere.

The proliferation of AA and NA has affected recovery treatment among differing ethnic and racial groups. In fact, many members of these groups have as their first AA or NA contact members of their own ethnic or racial group. This seems to support identification with others and helps to maintain addiction as the figure in the addict's awareness. Where there is enough identification with the cultural group, as in Gay and Lesbian groups, the recovering addicts can sometimes feel supported in becoming and remaining sober in their social or cultural context.

Differences in ethnic groups can also become figural in terms of spirituality and relationships with others. First, recovering addicts have already developed patterns of social and group interactions, deeply rooted in their own ethnic tradition. I attended a meeting of recovering alcoholics on a Navajo reservation, where the entire group belonged to the nation. What struck me was the long periods of silence during conversation, which they experienced as listening with respect. These were punctuated by periodic nods, often without words. This pattern of interaction is typical in the Navajo culture, in contrast to an East Coast white or African American meeting, where interaction is highly verbal and individuals rely on verbal feedback to stay sober. This illustrates how some aspects of recovery are culturally divergent.

Spirituality is itself embedded in some context or tradition. The form and understanding of each addict's transpersonal experience is influenced by the world in which that addict has lived. For some recovering addicts, issues of death and existential limitations may be clearly within the context of their ethnic religious experience. For others, the struggle may be to define their conception of God or spirituality in contrast to their ethnic group's definition and practices.

DIFFERENCES IN DRUG OF CHOICE

Throughout this book, I have stressed the belief that it does not matter what drug an addict uses: addiction is determined by *how* and *how much* the addict uses. My experience has been that separating types of addicts in treatment is nonproductive. Distinctions between alcoholics and drug addicts often support alcoholics to continue to have reservations about drug use and vice versa. I have also worked with and know numerous drug addicts who returned to their addiction through social drinking, and many alcoholics who returned to the bottle by using medications.

However, individual differences of the type of drug use do affect addicts' lifestyles and their cognitive, emotional, and social functioning. These differences also influence the type and frequency of interventions that are useful, depending on the stage and task of recovery. I will attempt to illustrate these differences here by discussing the type of drug used and its impact on the addict's stages of recovery as presented in this book.

   • *Alcohol and other depressant drugs tend to desensitize the user when taken extensively.* This desensitization seems to end soon after ending drinking or using. For the user of these drugs, early recovery is often experienced as "waking up." Depressant drug users can be like sleepwalkers who know they have been somewhere but are not fully aware of where or how they felt or what they did. Feelings of elation and relaxation were often provided by the drug, at least initially. In early recovery, these addicts have to develop supports to tolerate sensation and to become aware of the world around them.

   • *Amphetamines, cocaine, PCP, or other stimulants generally stimulate the entire central nervous system, influencing cognitive process.* They can have effects more dramatic than those of depressant drugs.

The addict can become suspicious and eventually paranoid, and this style of contact can persist for years after abstinence, depending on how long the drugs were used. Stimulant drug users need to slow down their pace so they can attend more fully. They frequently develop a kind of hyper scanning style of perception and thinking, sometimes to the exclusion of emotional awareness. A slow pace and appreciation of the brittle quality of their experience are important guidelines for the therapist.

Interventions that stimulate or increase anxiety should be avoided in early recovery therapy with these addicts. I have found it more useful to slow down the pace of the therapy by focusing on relaxation and grounding. Overstimulation can cause the stimulant addict to become suspicious, paranoid, and on alert for possible threats from the therapist. I encourage these clients to avoid using caffeinated drinks such as coffee and soft drinks. Lack of sleep or stimulation sometimes can give these addicts the experience of being mildly high.

• *Narcotic or opiate drugs eliminate pain of all sorts.* Perhaps as a result, their users have an extreme aversion to pain, particularly emotional pain. These drugs seem to cause less long-term physical damage than other substances. However, because of the culture associated with narcotic use, these addicts may have a history or pattern of criminal and illegal behavior, which leads to damage in itself. They sometimes view recovery groups as a sort of clean and sober gang or posse. These addicts may have extreme discomfort in more traditional social organizations and practices (church, synagogue, civic groups).

In contrast to stimulant drug users, the growing edge for narcotic addicts is to increase sensation. Returning to the Gestalt cycle, this edge is one of trying to remain confluent and have little sensation emerge. Stimulating or charging interventions can create the sensation (and anxiety) necessary for these clients to register their experience. They tend to prefer to remain in withdrawal from past experiences. In individual therapy, it is useful to remain aware of talking about feelings with these clients. Increased breathing and movement will support sensation, as will encouraging the use of first-person language, that is, of making "I" statements. I have found it useful to immediately confront any pattern of these clients' talking to me like I'm their street buddy. This will break the confluence and heighten their awareness of who they are in relation to me (and others).

• *Hallucinogenic drugs profoundly alter consciousness; users can develop a tendency to dissociate and even hallucinate even when not under the direct influence of the drugs.* The case study of Donna (in Chapter Five) is an excellent example of regression during some stress in recovery to a more dissociative state. I have found it important to use concrete, literal language with these clients and to focus on clear, behaviorally defined issues, rather than on such issues as "I want to know who I am" or "I'm here to find my inner child." If addicts are newly recovering, the emphasis in therapy should be on how they can stay in this reality. Empty chair work, visualizations, and use of imagery tends to loosen their guard, which can often be counterproductive.

Marijuana users may tend to be less prone to hallucinations of dissociative episodes but often have difficulty focusing in early recovery. They tend to be abstract and metaphorical in their thinking. Gestalt interventions such as use of metaphor or playing parts may be easy for them, but often lack the specificity and clarity necessary for change and awareness. The work with these clients, particularly in first-stage recovery, is to support solidity and concrete thinking.

The individual differences I have presented here are not exhaustive. Many other aspects of the self and environment influence the focus of therapy with recovering addicts. The differences in this chapter represent the most common types that I experience in practice. There are many others not discussed here, including the use and abuse of food, the repercussions of childhood abuse and adult combat, and the effects of more profound thought disorders such as schizophrenia.

All of these individual differences can be understood in terms of the recovering client's capacity to make contact with self and others. Our therapeutic work with each recovering client can be best understood through the lens of meaningful behavior. That is, we can understand the recovering addict's behavior only by appreciating the whole person and incorporating this whole into our clinical approaches at each stage of recovery.

Recommended Reading

Blume, S. (1985). Women and alcohol. In *Alcoholism and substance abuse: Strategies for clinical intervention.* New York: Free Press.

Caution, G. (1986). Alcoholism and the black family. In R. Ackerman (Ed.),

Growing in the shadow. Pompano Beach, FL: Health Communications.

Daley, D., Moss, H., & Campbell, F. (1987). *Dual disorders.* Center City, MN: Hazelden Foundation.

Greenberg, E. (1989). Healing the borderline. *Gestalt Journal, 12* (2), 11–55.

Jordan, J. (1991). Empathy and self boundaries. In *Women's growth and connection: Writings from the Stone Center.* New York: Guilford Press.

Levin, J. (1987). *Treatment of alcoholism and other addictions.* Northvale, NJ: Aronson.

Perls, L. (1992). *Living at the boundary.* Highland, NY: Gestalt Journal Press.

Yontef, G. (1993). *Awareness, dialogue, and process.* Highland, NY: Gestalt Journal Press.

CHAPTER NINE

Working with the Body

T he way recovering addicts experience their physical process can be a useful focus in therapy. This approach is a continuation of the self-modulation model based on the holistic belief that body *is* self. We are constantly modulating our experience through our body process. As I have described, there are patterns of modulation more common to addicts, such as desensitization and overstimulation. In this chapter, I offer some body-oriented interventions in working with these issues.

BODY AS MACHINE, BODY AS ENEMY

Part of the intention of the addict when using is to make the physical sensate experience constant, immutable to the variations of life. Nowhere is this more visible than in the way addicts relate to their body. Of course, even to speak about relating to the body is already to be one step removed. My body is not something I have, but *me*. But for the addict this separation is profound and takes two forms, body as a machine and body as an enemy.

In the early stages of drug use, an addict learns to separate self from sensation—from bodily pain, fear, longing, anger, and so on. This is because sensation and resulting feeling is inherently physical. By dephysicalizing or creating an on-demand chemical field of sensations, the addict treats the body like a mechanism. Like a mechanism to be given more or less additives to make it run smoothly, hence a machine. This view of our bodies as machines seems to be a tendency of our culture, with its emphasis on the proper medicine for *the* body, on *body sculpting,* on all the rituals we develop for ignoring our bodies. We say things like "my back is killing me" or "I've got to get my body in shape." Statements like these reflect a disconnection from body—as if I, in my body, am somehow separate from I, the speaker or thinker. For most of us, this sort of verbal separation marks a minor discontinuity that does little damage to our health. But the addict makes the distinction repetitiously, compulsively, and to the extreme. Also, the drugs addicts use create a further detachment of self and body.

Unlike a racing car or other finely tooled machine, the addict's body seems to want more and more gas and additives, eventually never having enough. It is then that the addict experiences the body as an enemy, a traitor who will not do what the addict wants. Heroin addicts often talk about feeding "it." They describe their experience as "chasing the dragon." These descriptions are of both the drug and the body—after a while, the addict perceives his or her body as a thing, separate from the self.

In early recovery and even in the later stages, addicts often continue to experience the body as something separate from "I." Now it is part of the disease, the new "it." I have frequently heard addicts and alcoholics talk about not being able to trust their body and their feelings. Feelings are both physical and accompanied by thoughts, but we experience our feelings as body sensations. To stop trusting feelings is to stop trusting our body sensations. This is often the result of years of desensitization, culminating in a body experience that surfaces only peripherally or in craving and withdrawal. Addicts use phrases like "It lies to me . . . I know what I am feeling but what is really true? . . . I can't trust my feelings, my feelings got me drunk." There is some truth in all of these statements, of course. At one time every addict felt that having another drink was a *great* idea, only to wake up the next day regretting that decision. What I am describing is the pervasive, lasting belief among recovering addicts that physical experience is a deception and somehow different from the self. The addict must learn to observe sensations so as to not give in to the craving.

As I discussed earlier, each addict needs to learn to inhibit or retroflect the desire to use. In retroflection, we split ourselves into two parts; a part or desire to act and a part or desire to inhibit the action. Often, addicts learn to inhibit their physical desire to use by *thinking the drink through.* But this self-talk can continue long into recovery, developing as an unaware process. That is, the addict can be unaware that he or she is not letting feelings other than the desire for drugs and actions flow in a normal self-regulating pattern. Their experience is one of thinking of the whole of their experience as foreign. The unexpressed, inhibited body experience becomes part of the disease polarity, not to be trusted. In a sense, the addict is desensitizing without using drugs, splitting off from feelings and thinking away sensations. An old recovering friend of mine used to call this process "alcollectualizing." Recovering addicts are at this point in first-stage recovery. The clinical challenge is to help the addict move through the task of developing sensation. To do this, the addict will have to feel him- or herself *as somebody*—often desirable but anxiety-producing. An example of this attitude will be helpful in illustrating the split between self and body common to addicts in early recovery.

WHAT IS MY BODY DOING TO ME?

Phil was sober for three years. He entered therapy because of his consistent feeling of anxiety. His first statement when I asked him what he wanted from therapy was, "I want to know what my body is doing to me! It seems like I can't control the feelings that happen when I talk to other people." Phil experienced his body as doing something to him and wanted to control what he felt. His feelings happened to him. The work with Phil involved helping him to experience his body as himself and to feel his feelings in relation to some event, person, or memory. In fact, what Phil discovered was that he was afraid of sounding stupid when talking to other people. He would hold his breath by squeezing his diaphragm, creating the physical sensations that he called anxiety. At one point in our work, Phil disclosed to me that he had thought about using drugs again to stop these feelings. As Phil became more aware of how he tightened himself (not his body) and then couldn't breathe, he was able to explore what he would feel if he didn't tighten himself. Phil breathed more fully and felt frightened. This led to his awareness that he was shamed as a child when he wore braces, so he kept his mouth shut. By developing sensations, Phil completed the cycle of contact that he had previously interrupted.

Phil's experience is typical of many recovering addicts who separate from their body experience, in a sense to avoid their pain and make it *the pain*. This is useful to them for some time but eventually creates the dichotomy described as body doing something to self. For the addict, even if recovering, the habitual response to such a foreign feeling is to drug it. The ultimate problem for addicts if they stay split is a return of the old means of modulating unwanted or uncomfortable feelings—drug it. This is why it is crucial for the recovering addict to become reacquainted with the body as self. This task for recovering addicts is to discriminate sensations. At one point in the addict's history, most sensations feel like a desire to use drugs. Hunger, anxiety, exhaustion all became reasons for using—pains to be "cured" by a drink, snort, pill, or shot. In recovery, these sensations are sometimes ignored or dismissed as cravings to use. Developing body sensations then becomes an important step for recovering addicts to regain their emotional range and explore the second stage of self in relation to others.

The recovering addict often experiences his or her body as separate from others, in a sense alienated. But we move in relation to others or inhibit our movements toward others because of possible outcomes we want to avoid. We experience contact with others in our body. The addict who has perfected separating self from others is often in the process of managing internal sensations.

BODY-ORIENTED TECHNIQUES IN THERAPY

As described by Jim Kepner and Edward Smith, there are a variety of body-oriented techniques or approaches that can be used with Gestalt therapy. The emphasis in a Gestalt-oriented body process is on restoring awareness, choice, and range of expression. The choice of intervention is guided by the recovering client's degree of connection with his or her own physical process. For example, with recovering clients in first-stage recovery, I tend to focus more on breathing and on the client's sense of physical groundedness. I encourage clients to notice their body sensations, and I support them to put language to these sensations.

Clients in second-stage recovery are often inhibited in relation to others, having previously relied on drugs to release their inhibitions. Other clients in this stage feel physically unempowered as they sit or stand in a collapsed or rigid posture. Physical stance and the sense of competency are related; clients feel their capacity to interact in the legs and spine. This kind of attention to physical posture is often useful in supporting the tasks of interpersonal competency. Expressive body-oriented therapy is useful in undoing old patterns and habituations, such as holding back grief or anger. These techniques are often useful in unfinished trauma or family-of-origin work, which emerges in the end of first-stage and throughout second-stage recovery. Attending to the recovering addicts' desensitized patterns in their bodies can help clients resolve and finish old experiences and begin to live more in the present.

One working goal I have often used in therapy with addicts is to help them become reacquainted with their bodies. This may sound like an obvious experience, since we all know where our bodies are, don't we? It isn't like we lost them along the way. Yet in a sense, this is exactly the case for many addicts. Becoming reacquainted with self as body is often as simple as feeling your back on the chair, noticing how you begin to breathe as you remember your last drunk, or experiencing sexual contact without being intoxicated. These are all new boundary experiences. The goal here is to develop body sensation and body awareness in the moment; in a sense, to come into one's self in the moment.

Breathing and Groundedness

Breathing is one aspect of what I call grounding. By *grounding*, I refer to feeling oneself in relation to the physical environment. Many addicts tend to intellectualize or abstract their experience, especially when anxious. In moving through the addicted cycle, they tend to move quickly, breathing in a rushed pattern, often overstimulating themselves. They create a faster habitual thinking and pace. The result of this is often a rushed awareness or feelings of being flooded with sensation.

Attention to breath is an effective way to create more sensation and feeling. Fuller breathing delivers more oxygen to the blood, enabling more sensation to develop. Fuller breathing can also relax and soften the muscles. In these ways, encouraging an addict to breathe more fully can support the client to slow down and also develop sensations into feeling awareness.

In early recovery, addicts frequently have difficulty relaxing without using drugs. During withdrawal, their muscles can stiffen in response to the absence of the drug. When I worked at a detoxification center, I helped clients learn how to relax during that period of tension and anxiety by teaching them deep abdominal breathing.

This procedure developed from an experience I had with William, a client who had been addicted to Miltown for many years and could not sleep or relax. He was frightened that he would have a convulsion, even though he was taking an anticonvulsant medication.

I sat down to talk with William at a table on a night when he couldn't sleep. As I listened to him, I became frightened that he would become so agitated that he might just bring about a convulsion. I could feel my own breathing as shallow and rapid. As he talked about his fear, I began to breathe as I'd been taught in yoga, slowly and deeply into my belly. Soon I felt relaxed and suggested that he join me, mostly because I didn't know what else to do—words were not making any difference. We practiced this together for about an hour. He eventually began to slow down his breathing, and to both of our relief, his thinking. He actually began to look tired. After another half-hour of breathing and talking, I suggested he lie down on his bed and try the breathing. When I checked on him again, he was sound asleep.

Two things came out of this experience. The first was that William learned he was agitating *himself* and could also relax himself, and thus relieve his own fear. He realized he could influence his bodily and mental experience *simply* by breathing. I saw him five years later and he was still sober. When he saw me, he patted his belly and laughed, "Breathe, buddy!" He clearly remembered the experience, and in fact studied yoga during his recovery. For me, the learning was something I incorporated into my work, teaching many clients to slow down and relax by fuller, deeper breathing. This is particularly helpful for clients in withdrawal or with anxiety and dissociation tendencies.

Another form of grounding is for the addict to feel him or herself in the room at the present moment. Recall the case of Betty (in Chapter Five). She had merged in her awareness with others and was able to differentiate by feeling her back as she sat in the chair in my office. We can help clients feel more grounded by making them aware of their contact with the floor or chair back, or by encouraging them to see the room around them. This sensory orientation can help clients experience the *context* or *ground* of the moment. I have found that recovering addicts have used these simple tasks of mindfulness to stay in the present and not project into the future. In one way, this process is the opposite of intoxication, where the present—the here and now—becomes blurred. This new process is sobering.

Increased breathing also supports recovering addicts to become more sensitized to themselves and others, to feel more keenly their own sensations and emotions and to sense the physical-emotional experience of others.

I FEEL SO OUT OF TOUCH

Mike is a recovering addict of fifteen years who came to therapy complaining of feeling "out of touch with myself." He wondered if he were depressed. I noticed by looking at Mike's chest and stomach that his breathing was shallow and slow. This made him look stiff as he spoke about his life and family. I told Mike the way in which I perceived his breathing. He was surprised (as many clients are when I comment on their physical behavior) and asked, "What does that mean?" I answered that I wasn't sure what it meant, but believed he might learn by experimenting with his breathing.

Mike agreed to do this and initially took deeper breaths, eventually filling up his chest and stomach on each inhale and emptying out on each exhalation. As he did so, Mike began to shudder and shake. I asked him if he could stay with this experience. After a few minutes, Mike began to modulate his breathing in a more rhythmic way. The sound that he made was like a moaning. Mike's chin shook and he began to cry. I asked him if there were words for his crying and he said, "I'm not sure." I suggested his words from the beginning of the session, "I feel so out of touch." He tried saying these words three times, each time filling his chest and tearing up, and then added, "And in so much pain. . . . That's it. I feel so out of touch and so sad about my life." We spent the rest of the session defining what about himself and others Mike was out of touch with.

As with Mike, we can help recovering clients develop an optional form of self-modulation and expression through their body processes. Mike had learned to keep himself out of touch by literally not taking in breath, yet he was unaware of this choice as we began our work. Over time, he had inhibited his breathing as a way to modulate his sadness, and this inhibition had become part of his assumed stance in the world. Our approach in therapy focused on developing sensation by undoing Mike's retroflective pattern of holding his chest and stomach tightly, thus decreasing his available body sensation.

The notion of confluence, described earlier as a lack of boundary, is a body process as well as an emotional one. It can create a confluent physical contact and a pseudofamiliarity. Many addicts in twelve step programs shake hands and hug each other upon meeting. These gestures are a means of contact, and can serve as grounding, enabling one person to experience another, to feel that other's presence in his or her field. Each person's experience is thereby made more substantial, in that the individual's physical self becomes more clearly defined in relation to another body. But often these encounters are rote, carried out with little feeling or awareness. I have felt the limpness or hurry in these contacts, which end up feeling to me nonsubstantial. It is as if the huggers are not in their bodies and don't feel who they are hugging. A verbal parallel is the familiar greeting of "How are you?"—where the person who asks the question has no intention of finding out how you are. It's the form of interest without the substance.

When I am approached by a recovering client who wants to hug me or shake hands, I am alert to the uniqueness of this kind of contact in each situation. I might agree to greeting a client through physical contact, depending on who that person is and what he or she brings to the encounter (abuse history, history of boundary violations by a therapist). I always suggest that we look at each other. A client of mine asked me why I suggested this and I answered, "Because I want to see who I am touching and who is touching me. A hug or a handshake are not grounding per se. What can be grounding is *hugging you* or *shaking your hand.*" My emphasis here is to encourage the addict to move the self outward in physical contact with others. In this way, we can appreciate each other and the addict can feel direct support and contact with another.

Expressive Work

Gestalt therapy techniques such as empty chair work, pillow pounding, and various expressive movements have long been employed in addiction treatment. While these interventions can sometimes be helpful, just as frequently the addict-client can leave the experience having discharged some emotion but unfinished with the theme, soon to feel the same theme reemerge. I have participated in marathon sessions, individual and group, where addicts have done this kind of work. While these activities can certainly be stimulating (which may be the attraction), clients frequently learn or change little through performing them. This lack of closure or integration from expressive work is due not to a lack of efficacy of physical expressive therapy, but to a therapist's appropriating part of a methodology without the whole.

The Gestalt approach to expressive work is based on two principles often neglected in these exercises: developing the expression or movement out of the client's natural, already existing movement, and attending to counter-movement or resistance. It is useful to explore the implications of these principles.

Natural Movement

The power of expressive work comes from what clients are already doing or not letting themselves do, whether it be to express anger, grief, or hurt. If a client touches his chest when he talks about feeling sad, then this movement of touching the chest is an expression of his feeling. I encourage him to continue to touch his chest while he speaks rather than to do something else.

Similarly, a woman client literally dug her heels into my rug when she thought about her alcoholic mother. Digging in her heels is what I am calling a natural movement; she was unaware of doing this until I observed and commented on the gesture, and asked her to dig her heels in intentionally as she pictured her mother. She did so repeatedly, until she was aware of *what she was doing:* digging in her heels at her mother's insistence that she agree to something. The value of developing and focusing her movement into an expression was that the gesture held enormous meaning for her; it was her stance in life with many people. She was often digging in her heels with others, yet had no sense of what people meant when they described her as stubborn. After this work, she was able to integrate the movement as an expression of her stance with her mother, and to choose whether she wanted to dig in her heels. It was useful for her to dig in her heels in certain situations; the key point here is her emerging awareness that supports choice.

These examples of experiments in working with clients' idiosyncratic gestures are ways to use the client's own experience by tapping into forms of inherent expression that carry meaning for the individual. In contrast, to ask all clients to perform the same movement designed by the therapist might certainly evoke sensations but often doesn't lead to new meanings. Movement is significant and has meaning when it is part of the client's present or inhibited expression.

Resistance or Counter-Movements

As discussed earlier, addicts frequently retroflect or inhibit feelings. That is, they have both a desire or feeling and a resistance to that feeling or to the action it may provoke. On a physical level, we can see this as movement and counter-movement. In expression, there is some kind of tension between these two movements, and such unresolved tension can result in headaches, breathing inhibition, or locked jaw. Yet it can also be a fertile point of exploration in expressive therapy.

Without a focus on this dynamic tension, expressive work often becomes a complaint, or an activity that leaves the addict-client feeling guilty or unable to follow through outside of therapy.

I remember watching a video of expressive work done to demonstrate anger work toward parents. Each participant pounded on pillows while talking as though to their parents, with encouragement by the leader to "get your feelings out." Initially, their movements were awkward and hesitant, but with further encouragement, most of the group became more intense in their movements and pounded the pillows with increasing vigor. These exercises are common in the everyday treatment of addiction, where they are often used to work through family-of-origin themes.

What was not addressed in this nationally televised demonstration was the participants' objections or resistance to feeling or expressing anger toward their parents. This was apparent in the way all these people inhibited their movements (tightening their shoulders, locking their arms or pelvis). These counter-movements are also expressions, not of the desire to pound the pillow, but of the opposite desire, to interfere with that expression of anger. The counter-movement is internally focused back toward the self, and may reflect the deeper conflict of being angry at parents and still not wanting to lose them, or even simultaneously wanting to hold them. This ambivalence is expressed in the addict's initial holding back, and in the eventual flurry of anger.

A method of working this fuller expression is to attend to the tension addict-clients express along with their feelings. When I have worked with clients in this way, I encourage them to give voice and movement to both sides of their experience: their desire to push away and their desire to hold close. Two means of expressing the counter-movement are for clients to perform an inhibiting gesture intentionally, such as tightening their arms, and simultaneously to put words to this inhibition, for example, "I can't let myself be angry with you." Or, "I must hold myself back from you or you'll know how I feel."

Expressing only one side does not capture the fullness of conflicted relationships. Addict-clients learned to inhibit their expression of feelings because such inhibition was useful at one time, or because their environment did not support their feelings. Because that learning served a purpose in the past, it needs specific attention to undo it now; it will not simply disappear. Here are some examples of movements and possible counter-movements that can more fully express the conflict of feelings:

- Moving arms outward toward another person versus tightening arms and shoulders in toward self
- Bringing sensation to eyes and face by breathing fully versus squeezing throat and holding breath
- Moving or stamping legs versus tightening legs
- Relaxing chest versus tightening or stiffening chest
- Opening hands versus clenching fists

Expressive therapy work can include each of these dichotomies. The full conflict exists in the tension between the two poles, the yes and no of the expression of any feeling. By putting words to the movements, the client can experience the emotion more fully than if the therapist simply decides what side of the polarity (expressing anger versus rejecting it, for example) is the right or healthy direction.

Attending to two supports for this kind of work in therapy will aid in development and integration of expressive work. First, as therapist I want to be familiar with or capable of performing the expressive movement myself before I help my client move through it. The mechanics of any movement are a helpful ground for me as I follow the client. One way to be familiar is to do the movement with the client.

A second piece I call follow-through. This can mean having clients try the movement a number of times to explore their range and to feel any way they might restrict or inhibit themselves. Following through can also be supported by asking questions like, "Do you feel satisfied . . . finished . . . or stopped?" These questions can help clients keep in contact with the experience of how they are expressing themselves and moving.

BODY WORK IN PRACTICE

The following examples illustrate working with the recovering client's body experience in therapy. In the first, the focus is on the client's movements with the emphasis on counter-movements and contactful expression. By contactful expression I mean a full attention to the *meaning* of the client's expression and conflicting feelings about that expression. The second illustrates the way recovering clients carry or *embody* their life experience. Body-oriented therapy can help clients articulate these experiences.

TERRI

Terri, a young woman, had been passive in a therapy group. She and the group had become aware of her behavior and the group encouraged her to push back at them when she stated that she felt like they were pushing her. She responded that she was interested in pushing back but didn't know how. The group developed an experiment in which she would literally push members who volunteered. Terri tried this with a few group members and looked stiff as she did so. I asked her if she felt satisfied and she said, "I want someone to push back." Another woman in the group volunteered to do this.

They began pushing against one another, and Terri became much more energetic. Twice during these interactions I asked her, "Are you satisfied?" and she said, "Not yet!"

Eventually, they ran out of energy. The interaction looked finished. I then asked Terri what the experience had been like, what happened when she pushed and someone pushed back. She said she initially hadn't wanted to push if she did it all alone but felt energized when she felt the equal force of her partner. She experienced that she could be what she called "pushy" and not hurt anyone.

This is an example of the dual qualities of any expressive work. This client had always needed a few drinks to assert herself and later felt guilty that she was experienced as a pushy woman, as if there were something inherently wrong with that. She was also left alone as a child and literally had no one to push against. She would give up, assuming a passive position, one that she returned to in life both verbally and in her body. In this experiment, she was able to explore her need to assert and follow through. Her story and dual theme became clear to her through the expressive work.

ANDREW

Andrew had the look of a man who was filled with grief. His eyes were heavy and he looked lost. He walked as if he were falling into the floor under an enormous weight on his back. He had been sober for about three years when he attended a workshop I was presenting for addiction therapists. Andrew had just begun graduate school and was excited about his new career. Nonetheless, he would always frown downward with his mouth and eyebrows when he spoke or looked at others; frowning seemed to be his natural pattern. He did this repeatedly whenever anyone in the workshop expressed some sadness or pain. I asked him about the expression and he replied that he was not aware of his face, but felt congested. I asked Andrew to pay attention to his face and to note if he detected any tension.

The next day he said he'd been reading his daughter a story and felt himself frown, and that he'd also frowned when he heard some music on the radio. I suggested that he exaggerate this movement and he did so a number of times. After the third time, Andrew's eyes began to tear up and he said, "I'm sad!"

Rather than immediately ask him what he was sad about, I asked Andrew to try that movement again. He said, "I will be squashing my tears."

This became the theme of work for Andrew: how he squashes his tears by tightening the muscles around his eyes. Andrew's tears were about the way he had hurt his daughter and others when he was drinking. He said he'd never felt them (or anything else) while he was drinking.

—⁓—

Andrew's experience is an example of how recovery addicts *embody* their pain and patterns of desensitization. These patterns continue into recovery and are natural movements or counter-movements. The undoing or unpacking of long-term body patterns is another step in the return to full-contact functioning in recovery from addiction.

The use of body-focused interventions with recovering addicts offers another option in helping these clients to develop sensations, pace and ground their contact with others and with self, and express inhibited or conflicted feelings that have become embodied.

These approaches can be used throughout the stages of recovery. However, early first-stage recovering clients, those maintaining abstinence and developing retroflections of the drug, will be most supported by grounding and breathing work. Second-stage recovery clients can make use of all of these approaches; in the second stage of recovery the physical expression and inhibition with others becomes more figural in therapy. In working with third-stage clients, the use of body-oriented meditative practices can support the reflective-contemplative and transcendence tasks. Frequently, addicts who have been abstinent for many years have managed that process by becoming detached from their body. This approach can provide these clients with a whole new awareness of feeling themselves in recovery.

Working with these body experiences of recovering addicts can also help heal the intense sense of shame that many of these clients feel and express. It can be a means of reacquainting them with their body self. Body-oriented therapy also allows the addict to develop choices of action and self-expression while honoring existing patterns. For the recovering addict, such normalization is the healing from years of self-alienation, shame, and guilt.

Recommended Reading

Kepner, J. (1987). *Body process.* Lake Worth, FL: Gardner Press.
Smith, E. (1985). *The body in psychotherapy.* Jefferson, NC: McFarland.

CHAPTER TEN

Further Applications of the Self-Modulation Model

he process of recovery from addiction as I've described it is a lens through which we can assess, understand, and treat recovering clients. The interventions described in this book are based on three observations about the nature of recovery. These observations provide the basis for an approach that understands recovery as more than maintaining sobriety.

The first observation is that the foundation of recovery is abstinence. As long as addicts continue to use and live in the addiction cycle, meaningful change and options of behavior are severely limited and made secondary to the dominant figure of the drug. It is the recovering addict's intolerance of sensation, grounded in shame, boredom, mistrust, and lack of confidence, that has been modulated through drugs. Without abstinence, this ground cannot be explored and worked through in therapy. Another part of this observation is my clinical experience that abstinence from all nonprescription drugs, without regard to the recovering addict's drug of choice, is the only true abstinence. I have no clinical or anecdotal data of addicts safely drinking or alcoholics safely using drugs without starting the addiction cycle again.

My second observation is that recovery is an expansion beyond the self-boundary to increasing interrelatedness with others and the world. To view recovery as an expansion is to see it as a movement in the opposite direction from the movement during addiction, which is toward self-preoccupation and narcissism. The work in therapy with recovering addicts is to attend to this expansion, work that may at times push the boundaries of the therapist's own comfort and development, as, for example, in working with the transpersonal task in later recovery.

The third observation is that recovery is not merely chronological but evolutionary. Recovering addicts can be abstinent for ten or twenty years and still focus exclusively on first-stage recovery, that is, merely on not drinking or using. When I use the term *long-term recovery*, I refer to the extent of the process of recovery rather than to the length of time an addict has been abstinent.

This model is important in its clinical applications. The self-modulation model provides three clinical advantages over the presently used disease model. First, it offers a stage-focused map of recovery, through which we can assess the recovering addict's level of progress and thus determine the corresponding therapeutic task of recovery. By understanding the addict-client's stage of recovery and relevant tasks, we can more accurately choose treatment interventions. The contact skills or recovery tasks relevant to the specific client's level of recovery become the focus of therapy. Focusing on and supporting the client's relatedness in different levels of system allows us to move the therapy out of the narrow, narcissistic world of the self in isolation. In this way, therapy provides an alternative to the addict's style of self-focus and helps the addict restore or develop contact skills with self, family, groups, and greater community.

The third clinical contribution of this approach is that it can bring a focus on the individual as unique and self-organizing back into the foreground of addiction treatment. As with much of the therapeutic community, the addiction treatment field has tended toward a reductionist approach. That is, we often reduce individuals to a singular type, ignoring or deemphasizing specific differences. While it may be helpful in early recovery to emphasize commonalties, particularly in educating clients to addiction, it is the individual person, embedded in social, cultural, developmental, and gender-related fields, that we face in our office. And it is this recovering person's unique struggle and integration into these fields that is the long-term work in recovery. When actively using drugs, addicts behave in a routinized habitual pattern, eventually experiencing few choices or new experiences. By contrast, recovery offers awareness, choice, and growth. By attending to a recovering addict's unique movement through the stages of recovery, we can maximize that individual's awareness, choice, and experience.

IMPLICATIONS FOR ADDICTION TREATMENT

Throughout this book, I have described treatment approaches in working with recovering addicts. These approaches are grounded in my understanding of recovery as an expanding boundary based on self-development, and on the addict's behavior in addiction and recovery as self-modulation. I feel it also important to discuss the implications of such a model for all addiction treatment.

How would this model change the focus of present addiction therapy? First, many therapists currently working with recovering clients may not consider the client's recovery from addiction important. An example of this is an esteemed colleague of mine who asks clients how long it has been since they used drugs, and if it is over ten years, he considers drug use a dead issue. It is interesting to me that he does not ask clients how they understand themselves in relation to recovery. I bring this up not as a corrective for this therapist but as an example of the general bias among therapists. Clearly, there is a counter-bias to this—other addiction therapists frame all aspects of the client's life as addiction and recovery.

I believe that the implication of the model I have presented is that the tendency toward the addiction cycle is crucial to a client's history, in terms of the impact of that tendency on the person's development and its potential to influence his or her present mode of contact. If a client becomes abstinent after using addictively for twenty years, his or her physical, emotional, and psychological patterns are not instantly restored to some predrug state. A parallel is the lasting effect on contact functioning of all levels of Posttraumatic Stress Disorder, whether from combat or from physical or sexual abuse. Similarly, the lifestyle that many addicts lead during their active use (which may include criminal behavior, chronic lying, or sexual behaviors inconsistent with their own moral and ethical beliefs) is often the unfinished business those clients bring to therapy. These are only some of the experiences addicts live with and bring to therapy, experiences that change the way they look at both world and self. Many of these behaviors are beyond the experiences of therapists, at least at the level and frequency at which addicts have engaged in them. Addicts are also likely to have been raised in a family where addiction is present, so that their early development may have been influenced by the same impulsive and unintegrated actions and sensations that they later engage in while using drugs. This family-of-origin experience is also what the addict in second- and third-stage recovery may bring to therapy.

Another clinical implication is an awareness of the recovering addict's tendency to engage in desensitized behavior such as talking about or intellectualizing feelings instead of experiencing them. Educational approaches in working with clients are useful in the early recovery but may effect little change, as in Toni's case (in Chapter Seven). Recovering addicts in twelve step programs tend to have extensive practice in talking about self, a behavior that at times can be another avoidance of self. The implication of this approach is that we need to attend to recovering clients' experience of self in therapy and to our own tendency to engage with them in intellectualizing about addiction.

Because recovery is the constant interplay between self and others, it is important for clinicians to be flexible about the level of system that we make the focus of therapy. Therapy that focuses exclusively on intrapersonal or self work may not be useful to a recovering addict in the second and third stage of recovery, in that it may only serve to perpetuate the addict's tendency toward isolation and narcissism.

On the other hand, with recovering addicts in the first stage of recovery, emphasizing systematic approaches without an awareness of the individual's intolerance of sensation or limited capacity for interpersonal contact may overload the client, or require him or her to desensitize in order to participate. When this occurs, the recovering client merely goes through the motions of recovery. The critical clinical judgment we must make is to match the recovering client's present level of recovery to the relevant treatment modality. Part of this assessment may be to determine what type of group or educational experience we might suggest to the client.

This model of recovery emphasizes the importance of transpersonal and spiritual relatedness as an important aspect of development in recovery. In fact, if they are not dissuaded by the therapist, many recovering addicts may bring this theme to therapy. This suggests, for me, that as therapists we need to attend to these themes with our clients from their perspective rather than from our own. In my own practice, I don't proselytize about my own spiritual beliefs, nor do I dismiss my clients through psychological criticisms such as projection or transference. I respect their spiritual beliefs as needs like any other. One of the ways that we can support this kind of interaction is to familiarize ourselves with the client's belief system, through reading or through conversation. We don't need to decide what is spiritually or psychologically true for our clients; rather, as with all of our clients' concerns, we can support their spiritual connections.

IMPLICATIONS FOR
TREATMENT DELIVERY SYSTEMS

The stages and tasks outlined here include work in groups, couples, and families. In particular, second-stage recovery tasks might best be supported clinically in group, couples, or family therapy. Some of the family-of-origin or mutual reparation work would also ideally take place in those types of therapy. But these options are not always available for a variety of reasons, ranging from inadequate funding to lack of availability to unwillingness of partners or family members to be involved in therapy.

I want to suggest some options for working with recovering addicts at these stages when such constraints make only short-term or individual therapy available. Individual therapy can be a useful lens *if* we, as therapists, are willing to attend to ourselves as part of a dyadic system. We are the client's significant other in the room. We offer the best resource in the moment for him or her to practice contact skills as well as to develop self-modulation skills. We can be a source of input into how clients interact, and can provide a forum for them to practice expression of anger, to feel empowered, or to listen to others. By offering ourselves as part of the client's process, and as part of a cocreated process, we can shift the focus of the work away from the client in isolation and toward the client and therapist as an interpersonal field. As both Gordon Wheeler and Robert Stolorow and George Atwood describe, this is only an acknowledgment of what already exists in therapy, the "we" of the therapist-client field. Some specific questions that arise out of this interpersonal approach to therapy are: How does the client maintain a boundary with the therapist? How does the client communicate his or her needs? What kind of relationship do the client and therapist create, and how is that similar or dissimilar to the client's present family or couple system? If we are to make use of these questions, we as therapists must attend to our own feelings, thoughts, and behaviors with the client.

Some other tasks of recovery can be supported in therapy, allowing the client to pursue them between sessions. These might be include readings in meditation or reflection that would support the client in developing those capacities. Most of us do not develop these capacities in ourselves, or attempt to become experts in spiritual matters only in our roles as therapists, but we can learn enough to support the client's pursuit of these levels.

When faced with a limited number of sessions, I have helped clients devise experiments to try between sessions, using the following sessions to try the experiment again or to process their experience outside of therapy. An example of this is a client who developed the idea of saying how he felt to people without censoring, and who had only six sessions available to him through his managed care company. In one session, we created a list of people he might do this with. In the following session, he told me what he'd experienced in actually carrying out this experiment, and then made some statement to me without censoring. With more time available, I might have explored this experiment during the session, using empty chairs, or with me enacting the role of someone else in his life.

The major implication of this approach for residential or hospital-based treatment is a shift away from the currently favored generic approach—"all addicts are the same"—toward a more individual emphasis. This is particularly true in terms of helping addicts in early recovery to develop alternative self-modulations. More emphasis will need to be given to aspects of self and of the client's ground (such as personality structure, ethnicity, race, and gender). This may be difficult as available treatment time continues to shrink. However, widening the lens to include these aspects of the client's ground can only help the client be seen in a fuller frame.

If group therapy can be made available, another alternative process can be to develop ongoing therapy groups for recovering addicts in second- and third-stage recovery. These might be groups focused on addicts during the first five years, or on long-term recovering addicts. Groups focusing on specific tasks and themes such as boundary setting and interpersonal competency could provide forums for these recovering addicts to normalize and work on this process.

The work with recovering addicts can be extended in ways like those described here. The major implication is that we, as clinicians, focus our attention on the process of recovery from addiction as part of the ongoing growth of some of our clients. Recovery is more than an alternative to addiction. In its fullest evolution, recovery is a restoration or development of self-functions and a reintegration into the world of others.

IMPLICATIONS FOR TREATMENT OF OTHER COMPULSIVE STYLES

The focus of this book has been the process of addiction to alcohol or drugs and the process of recovery from that addiction. An important consideration in the development of this model and approach is how it might apply to other compulsive disorders. I want to comment briefly on these as part of concluding this discussion. Some of this material and model may be applied to other so-called addictions, but I believe there are significant differences between other compulsive behaviors and drug and alcohol addiction and recovery. Some of these syndromes are presently defined as addictions in diagnostic manuals, and even more are being treated as such in practice and theory.

The American Psychiatric Association includes alcohol and drug dependence as substance disorders, overeating as an eating disorder, and pathological gambling as an impulse disorder. The term *substance dependence* is used equivocally for addiction, but the criteria for pathological gambling are similar to alcohol and drug dependence. Patrick Carnes describes compulsive sexual behavior as "sexual addiction" and as a progression of sexual behaviors modeled on the progression of alcoholism. He presents the twelve steps of AA as the treatment for sexual addiction.

Overeaters Anonymous is also based on an addiction model and applies the same twelve steps developed by AA, emphasizing the concept of powerlessness. That group has been splintered into two subgroups, differing mostly in their approach to recovery, with one favoring a more structured and disciplined recovery program.

According to Stanton Peele, we live in a culture where an increasing number of behaviors are defined as addiction. Peele calls this process the "diseasing of America." The proliferation of these groups suggests that the process he describes is accurate. But the major clinical concern I face when considering how this model may be applied is whether the various disorders are similar enough for the model to be useful. Three questions may clarify this concern, while leaving it to others to apply the model to treat other kinds of addictions:

- How far can we stretch the definition of addiction before it loses precision and practicality as an organizing frame of understanding and treating behavior?

- What are the specific individual and group differences among these addictions that might arise in applying the self-modulation model?

- How do these addictions differ in the stages of recovery and definition of abstinence?

ADDICTION AND RECOVERY AS BOUNDARY PHENOMENA

The Gestalt model of addiction is based on the view of contact with substances and people as boundary phenomena; that is, we experience others and substances at the boundary of self. Boundary is the edge or distinction of what is me and what is not me, what we call *us* or *our group* versus *not us* or *not our group*. Recovery from substance dependence is based on defining this boundary with the drug as keeping it outside of the self. This is abstinence. For drug addicts and alcoholics, abstinence is a clear and consistent boundary; there is no ambiguity. This clarity in regard to abstinence is the first task of the first-stage recovery process.

In contrast, this definition is not as distinct for other so-called addictions. It is impossible for a compulsive overeater to not take in food. For overeaters, the management of their compulsive behavior must be accomplished while *using the substance*. Many clients who are in OA talk about struggling with the multiple definitions of abstinence they encounter at meetings. Some define abstinence as amount of food or frequency of eating. Others define specific foods as the addictive substances (white flour, sugar) and do not use these foods. This variety of boundaries with food has a far greater diversity that the boundaries perceived by alcoholics and drug addicts. The struggle for many of these clients is that they often don't have the shared experience of abstinence as those in AA and NA do. According to Geneen Roth, the additional struggle for many who abuse food is the complexity of emotional needs for which food may serve as a substitute.

Despite these boundary questions, food addiction is what we might distinguish as a substance addiction. In contrast, we might define gambling, compulsive spending, and compulsive sex as process addictions. That is, the habituation is to the process and behavior rather than to the substance. They all can create some stimulation and euphoria. Each of these processes can be socially isolating and if continued can lead to the narrowing identified in the stages of addiction. Substance addiction can change awareness due to the use of the substance, and over time, can cause physiological and psychological damage. Process addictions likewise can change awareness, creating dependence on changes in body chemistry that result from the sensations associated with the behavior and that also result in long-term physiological and psychological damage. The impact goes beyond the observable repetition of the behavior.

Sexual addiction is another polymorphous definition. According to Patrick Carnes and Sex and Love Anonymous, the symptoms range from chronic masturbation, exhibitionism, and voyeurism to compulsive sexual interactions with others. Although there are some individuals who lead celibate lives, sexual drive is a normal aspect of human experience. Again the question arises, what is abstinence for sexual addicts? My clinical experiences have shown me that clients struggle with the question. Some definitions of abstinence that clients use include monogamy, looking at others without considering sexual attraction, avoiding masturbation, and engaging only in sexual behaviors that are grounded in contact with another person and based upon intimacy rather than using others as objects or inspirations for fantasy. I have heard clients struggle with these definitions and how to incorporate them into their lives. I believe that this confusion reflects the diversity of sexual behaviors presently being diagnosed as sexual addiction.

In my clinical experience, abstinence from gambling is a clearer boundary phenomenon: one either gambles or does not. There is no organismic need to gamble; it does not support the nurturance and survival of the self. Initially, it is a form of stimulation. I believe it to be a process that substitutes for other interactions or eventually replaces all other forms of stimulation, becoming the dominant figure. Recovery is also a clear boundary phenomenon; the gambler does not pick up the first betting slip, card, die, or whatever.

Some alcoholics and drug addicts are also compulsive gamblers and may substitute this process before or during recovery. This will interfere with their movement through the stages of recovery and will continue to narrow their awareness. Gambling during recovery from drug or alcohol addiction can keep the addict locked into a shortened cycle similar to that associated with using drugs or alcohol.

RECOVERY

I believe there are significant differences in the recovery process from these various addictions, differences that are apparent in the stages and tasks of recovery, and that suggest different clinical responses. The stages of recovery presented here are based on the alcohol and drug addict's tendency to internalize instead of moving outward into the environment and to avoid awareness through desensitization.

Recovery for alcoholics and drug addicts is based on the definite boundary of relation to the drug and the need to retroflect actions toward the drug. For other compulsive disorders or addictions, the developmental movement in recovery may be different. For example, the self-defined sexual addict may need to develop more internal awareness or basic contact skills with others as preparatory steps for contactful sexual interaction. For the drug addict and alcoholic, by contrast, developing internal awareness is not a preparatory step to drinking or using again. The difference lies in the alcoholic and drug addict's boundary with the drug as permanent and physiological. The goal of recovery work in drug addiction is not the restoration of intimate contact with the substance.

Food addicts need both to manage their overeating and to attend to their actual need for proteins, vitamins, and so on. Drug addicts or alcoholics do not need the chemicals in alcohol, cocaine, or heroin. My clinical experience is that there are differences between drug addicts and compulsive overeaters. I am focusing here on overeaters; anorexics and bulimics seem to evolve out of different developmental grounds. Overeaters tend to have porous boundaries; they are easily hurt or affected and tend to orient environmentally. They may need to strengthen self-boundaries and to diminish interpersonal dependency; separation and individuation seem to be more crucial with overeaters in early recovery work.

The later stages of recovery for food addicts are similar to the model presented here, but the key themes are the resolution of body image and body dysmorphia. The complexities of development and particularly women's development are more diverse than the model presented here. With recovering alcohol and drug addicts who also abuse food, the clinical focus needs to be on the individual's developmental needs in recovery.

Gambling addicts will follow through the stages of recovery as described here. There will be less physiological recovery than with alcohol and drug addiction. What may be useful is to explore the recovering gambler's return to social interaction through the larger levels of system as defined here. The first-stage task of retroflecting the desire for gambling is a crucial part of the recovery process, as is avoiding situations that might evoke the desire to gamble.

The process of any of these addictions will interfere with the development of other feelings and diminish awareness. Recovery will involve learning to stay with the feelings that have previously been avoided or desensitized.

—⁓—

We are at a place in our culture where we are beginning to examine our excesses. Defining many of these behaviors as addictions is part of that large social reframing. We live in a different social context from the 1960s, when excessive sexual and drug behavior were considered the norm by many people. The question on a larger level is what is middle ground or normal sexual, eating, or gambling behavior.

From a Gestalt perspective, *normal* can be defined as that which supports the healthy functioning of the self within the larger social context—not always an easy resolution for the individual. That some of these behaviors may not be correctly defined as addictions does not diminish the usefulness of some aspects of this model. They only become problematic when clinicians and clients ignore some of differences and try to treat everything as if it were alcohol and drug addiction.

FINAL THOUGHTS

A colleague remarked to me upon reading my original draft of this project, "When does it end? When does it stop being recovery and become life?" At the end of this book, my answer to this question is that recovery ends when the person in question no longer sees him or herself as a recovering addict—when he or she no longer organizes the field in this way. And yet, the way in which we organize the field is partially based on our history. The difference, then, is to what degree the client defines him or herself in terms of addiction and recovery. To answer the question from my perspective, *what is recovered is life.* What is recovered are the options of developing self and relatedness to others, and that kind of expansion doesn't ever need to end. I believe that for recovering addicts this growth is based on the tasks of developing a boundary with drugs, but that the long-term work is not about drugs; it is about self and others. So, to finally answer the question, maybe recovery is the addict's lifelong healing and development of self.

My hope is that this book provides a useful shift in the field of addiction treatment. It is meant to be provocative—the model I've presented here is considerably different from the prevalent disease model. The significant difference is that to look through the lens of self-modulation rather than through the lens of epidemiology brings the individual and his or her struggle into focus. These struggles are what we see every day in our offices, at clinics, or in group rooms. But some of what we as therapists have swallowed or taken in as gospel about addiction treatment may not fit the individuals we see.

I believe this is the ultimate test of the validity or usefulness of any model: how this approach fits the person, rather than how the person fits the model. I leave it to the reader to see how the observations fit in practice.

Recommended Reading

American Psychiatric Association. (1980). *Diagnostic and statistical manual of mental disorders.* (3rd ed., revised). Washington, DC: Author.

The Augustine Fellowship, Sex and Love Addicts Anonymous. (1986). *Sex and Love Addicts Anonymous.* Boston: Fellowship-Wide Services.

Carnes, P. (1983). *Out of the shadows.* Minneapolis, MN: CompCare.

Overeaters Anonymous, Inc. (1980). *Overeaters Anonymous.* Torrance, CA: Author.

Peele, S. (1991). *The diseasing of America.* San Francisco: New Lexington Books.

Roth, G. (1993). *Feeding the hungry heart.* New York: Penguin Books.

Stolorow, R., & Atwood, G. (1992). *Contexts of being: The intersubjective foundations of psychological life.* Hillsdale, NJ: Analytic Press.

Wheeler, G. (1991). *Gestalt reconsidered.* Lake Worth, FL: Gardner Press.

—ᴧᴧ— About the Author

Michael Craig Clemmens is a psychologist in private practice specializing in addiction recovery, body-oriented therapy, and abuse and trauma healing. He is a faculty member of the Gestalt Institute of Cleveland, where he teaches and chairs the specialization in working with individuals.

Clemmens has taught Gestalt and addiction treatment both nationally and internationally. His training includes phenomenological psychology, Gestalt therapy, and various body-oriented approaches to development. He was trained at the Institute in Cleveland and with other Gestalt trainers, including Lore Perls. He received his Ph.D. degree in 1987 from the University of Pittsburgh.

Clemmens lives in the Pittsburgh, Pennsylvania, area with his wife, Denise, and his two children, Lindsey and Brenden.

Index